Critical Race and Education for Black Males

This book is part of the Peter Lang Education list.
Every volume is peer reviewed and meets
the highest quality standards for content and production.

PETER LANG
New York • Bern • Berlin
Brussels • Vienna • Oxford • Warsaw

Vernon C. Lindsay

Critical Race and Education for Black Males

When Pretty Boys Become Men

PETER LANG
New York • Bern • Berlin
Brussels • Vienna • Oxford • Warsaw

Library of Congress Cataloging-in-Publication Data

Names: Lindsay, Vernon C., author.
Title: Critical race and education for Black males: when pretty boys
become men / Vernon C. Lindsay.
Description: New York: Peter Lang, 2018.
Includes bibliographical references and index.
Identifiers: LCCN 2018008093 | ISBN 978-1-4331-5460-7 (hardback: alk. paper)
ISBN 978-1-4331-5459-1 (paperback: alk. paper)
ISBN 978-1-4331-5461-4 (ebook pdf)
ISBN 978-1-4331-5462-1 (epub) | ISBN 978-1-4331-5463-8 (mobi)
Subjects: LCSH: African American boys—Education. | African American young
men—Education. | Critical pedagogy—United States. | Discrimination in
education—United States. | Racism in education—United States. |
Lindsay, Vernon C.
Classification: LCC LC2731.L56 | DDC 371.829/96073—dc23
LC record available at https://lccn.loc.gov/2018008093
DOI 10.3726/b13367

Bibliographic information published by **Die Deutsche Nationalbibliothek**.
Die Deutsche Nationalbibliothek lists this publication in the "Deutsche
Nationalbibliografie"; detailed bibliographic data are available
on the Internet at http://dnb.d-nb.de/.

This work was inspired by my family and every Black boy who I have ever mentored; you give me hope and without you this would not be possible.

TABLE OF CONTENTS

A POETIC PREFACE

I am one

I am male.
I am Black.
I am a Black male and so much more,
So much more than what you are about to explore.
This work takes you on a tour from my home on Chicago's Southside to the burbs.
Where I was the only boy, yes the one Sun, brother to five sisters, and a preacher's kid.
Emery and Pearl Lindsay's one.
The one who is married to one woman.
The one father to two sons and one daughter.
I am the one who fights for unity in the spirit of Marcus Garvey.
I am one with the beauty and strength of the Black community.
I am more than the tattoos that cover my body and the Black dreads that hang past my waist.
Much more than the three letters that appear behind my name.
Read on as I lift the veil to uncover the intricacies of race, racism, gender and masculinity,
With intentionality I want you to see One of many experiences of Black males born in America.

ACKNOWLEDGMENTS

There were some late nights and far too many early mornings in the process of creating this manuscript. I would like to first recognize The Creator for guiding and providing me with the strength, patience, and discipline to achieve this goal.

This book would not have been possible without an incredible partner and three amazing children who I am blessed to call family. You pushed me every day to strive for excellence as a husband, father, entrepreneur, and Black man. Thank you, Gabriella, Vizuri, Emery, and Mkazo for your support and presence in my life. I love you.

Thank you, David Stovall, Kerry Ann Rockquemore, Bill Ayers, Anthony Ocampo, Kendall Ficklin for offering me publishing advice, taking the time to respond to my emails, reviewing drafts of this project, and encouraging me throughout this journey. Your support meant the world to me.

Thank you to my external editors Badia Ahad and Jennifer Gavacs for reading early drafts and providing the critical feedback that was necessary to improve this book. Your feedback and recommendations were critical to the clarity I found through this work.

Thank you Peter Lang Press, for your support in this process and agreeing to publish this work.

Lastly, I would also like to acknowledge my parents and my sisters. Thank you for your consistent love, support and beliefs in me.

INTRODUCTION

I was sitting in the car outside of the Chicago daycare my children attended when I first received the news that set me on this path to move from the United States to live in Mexico and finish this book. My queen and wife was the first person to tell me about the murder of Michael Brown at the hands of a White police officer in Ferguson, Missouri. As she described the incident to me, my heart began to race, and the blood in my body filled with rage. The video of Brown's uncensored corpse face down in the street was all over Facebook, and as she finished explaining to me the reported details, she asked me if I had a chance to see it. My response was no, and I didn't want to see it because I knew I wouldn't be able to break that memory from my consciousness.

She exited the car to pick up the children, and I decided to "man-up" and log-in to Facebook to see the viral video of Brown's fatal body in the middle of the street. Without knowing much of the details, I was infuriated, shocked, disturbed, and concerned. In the weeks and months following Brown's murder, protests took place in every major city. I participated in and organized some of Chicago's marches because I was outraged by the vigilante mentality reinforced through racism that penetrated law enforcement and cut the life short of another young Black (Black is used throughout the text, because I find it more inclusive of the African diaspora than African-American) male. As a Black male and father to two Black boys, I was also concerned about the future of our lives and felt compelled to take action against the injustice. Michael Brown's murder hit home for several reasons.

I like Brown am a Black male who was born in the United States. Through my roles as a father and teacher of Black boys, I have a personal and professional relationship with others who are similar to Brown. I have experienced "random" traffic stops and other negative interactions with police officers, because of my physical appearance rather than the belief that I committed a crime. The young men whom I have taught and mentored have endured similar unpleasant experiences with the police. What happened to Brown could have happened to me or any of the other Black males with whom I have invested time, love, energy, and support.

The countless cases similar to Michael Brown have created anger and feelings of displacement among me and other Black males in a country we call home. In the United States, too often Black males are underserved by the public, private, and charter schools and over served by the criminal justice system. Such inequalities have led to underemployment, limited educational opportunities, false indictments, and in some cases murder by the police. This book is an intentional effort to give voice to Black males and their experiences with race, racism, and masculinity in search for an authentic self and full life.

Critical Race Theory

In my first semester of graduate school at the University of Illinois at Chicago, I took a course called "Critical Race Theory in Education." Derrick Bell's book, *Faces at the bottom of the well: The permanence of racism*, exposed me to the use of narratives to explore intersections between race, racism, and power. As a student in this course, I was also assigned to read several chapters from Dixson and Rousseau's edited book, *Critical race theory in education: All God's children got a song*, which furthered my interest in the theoretical framework to explore the contemporary implications of racism in education. The theory, methodologies, and approached used to report data I found in the *Critical Race Theory in Education* course enabled me to make better meaning of my experiences and other young Black males in schools.

Critical race theory is a paradigm and a movement of scholars invested in understanding the connections between race, racism and social inequalities. It is a derivative of critical legal studies with origins in the 1970s among students, researchers, lawyers, scholars, and activists invested in writing about and taking other actions against racial injustices (Cho & Westely, 2002; Corbado, 2011; Crenshaw, 1995, 2011; Delgado, 2000; Delgado & Stefancic, 2000, 2001; Harris, 2001). Narratives by people of color are one of many valid tools used to illustrate experiences that are uniquely shaped by the intersections between race and racism (Ladson-Billings & Tate, 2006; Parker & Lynn, 2002; Stovall, 2013; Yosso, 2006). Furthermore, narratives possess the power to create awareness of social inequalities and to inspire change.

This work is a series of brief autobiographical narratives that draw on critical race theory to explore my educational and other social experiences as a Black male born in the United States. Throughout the text, I deliberately use Black as opposed to African-American, because it conveys race and is applicable to people of African descent born throughout the diaspora. African-American is an ethnic term imposed on people who are racialized in the United States. This book shares stories from my experiences in grammar school, middle school, high school, college, and graduate school with the intention to offer recommendations that can apply to improving educational environments for Black boys and other young men of color.

To reflect the literature of critical race theory and to remain authentic to my experiences as a Black male, highlighted within each chapter is the influence of race and racism. However, as Tyrone Howard (2014) supports, it is essential to use the paradigm of critical race theory coupled with an analysis of gender to fully explore the experiences of Black males in education. Male, boy, and young man are interchangeably used throughout the text in reference to myself and others who subscribe to many of the culturally accepted gender norms of identity. This book is about the impact of race and gender on the life of someone who identifies as a Black cisgender man.

Occasionally, pseudonyms are used to protect the identities of my family members, friends, associates, teachers, and colleagues in the narratives offered in this text. Formal interviews were not conducted with any person who is mentioned in the chapters of this book. The stories reflect my memories of the dialogue and experiences as described within the text. To the best of my ability, they are factual and validated under the critical race theory in education framework which affirms the voices of people of color as a valid form of evidence to illustrate the permanence of racism.

With an analysis that explores race, gender, and masculinity constructs this book is a tool to help guide the creation of positive self-awareness in young Black males and other young men of color. My intention is to inspire changes within school cultures and school polices that can extend beyond lip service and make a measurable impact in communities of color.

What can you expect?

Although I ultimately earned a PhD in Policy Studies in Urban Education, I experienced some of the same challenges many young Black males encounter in school. In middle school and high school, I was suspended and forced to serve detentions. I had a high school counselor tell me I was unprepared and unfit to attend college. As an undergraduate student, I failed courses, and in graduate school, I faced accusations of stealing research from an esteemed professor. It is for these reasons that when I graduated with a PhD, I stood on the stage with my right fist in the air as a salute to my ancestors who endured great struggle for an education and as a testament to the traps I managed to sidestep along my journey.

From my youth to adulthood, I wrestled with the person I am and the person who I believed others wanted me to be. I fought other boys, stole merchandise from stores, and had poor relationships with girls as attempts to fit an accepted norm of masculinity. As a Black male with lighter skin who was called Yellow, I felt a strong desire to prove that I was just as Black as my peers. I played into negative stereotypes of Black manhood and embodied beliefs that the best options for my life included gangs, sports, or a career in entertainment. Black male identity is not limited to organized crime, professional athletics or positions in Hollywood, but in my youth, they had a much stronger appeal to me than my father's occupation as a Christian minister.

Me and my five sisters were raised in the church. On Sunday, Wednesday, and occasionally Saturdays we attended Christ Temple Cathedral located on the Southside of Chicago behind the Roseland Community Hospital. As a PK (Preacher's Kid) and the only son, there were many expectations imposed on my life. I was supposed to be well-behaved, a model student in school, and inevitably a pastor just like my father.

Despite others expectations for me as a PK, I wanted to carve a path in life that was in some ways contradictory to the teachings of the church. Gospel music did not have the same relevance and impact in my life as Hip-Hop. I was a big Tupac Shakur fan and of any rapper who I believed reflected my experiences as a young Black male growing up in urban America. The church preached modesty in dress and behavior. I sagged my pants and frequently got into trouble at school.

As a child, friends, and family teased me because I was short and "light skinned." At points in my life, I looked for my confidence through sports performances, gang affiliation, and poor romantic relationships with the opposite sex. Over the years, I learned how to turn my feelings of self-doubt, uncertainty, and confusion into a more positive and optimistic approach toward life. In my adulthood, I embraced a new outlook that enabled me to live life on my terms and with a vision to reach other Black males.

The book you hold in your hands illustrates my journey from my birth as a Black male, adolescence as a Black boy, and eventually to adulthood as a Black man. It discusses the concepts I learned in route to understanding my potential in life. It makes use of my story to illustrate how race, racism, and perceptions of gender influenced my decisions in school and other life choices including the decision to leave the United States with my wife and three small children to live in Mexico. The goal of this book is to assist educators in their efforts to provide a relevant education that can foster social consciousness and positive self-awareness among Black males. Educators can use this book as a resource to develop strategies that can aide Black males as they strive toward a better life for themselves, their families, and communities.

What is race? What is masculinity? How can we help Black males develop positive self-perceptions? In Chapter 1, *Birth of a Pretty Boy*, I begin with my early years on the Southside of Chicago in the Chatham community where I was initially socialized to understand my role in society as a young Black male. I discuss how growing up in a racially segregated city with a father who was a pastor, a mother who was a homemaker, and five sisters shaped an early vision of myself. This first narrative also describes the origin of the nickname Yellow Monkey that one of my sisters gifted me as a child. This chapter provides insight into how the communities of some Black males can influence the performance of socially constructed identities in school.

Chapter 2, *The Girl in the Pink Bikini*, provides the narratives of my first memories with racism. It makes use of my fourth-grade year in school, where I received ample requests for parent-teacher conferences and took a memorable spring break trip to Florida. My story reveals how I began to understand myself as a Black male in response to the perceptions people from outside my community imposed on me. The goal of this chapter is to illustrate how individual beliefs are the products of systemic racism and how opportunities for Black males to share their experiences can facilitate changes in school policies and school cultures.

In Chapter 3, *The Thug and Me*, is the story of my transition from life in Chicago to a south suburb called South Holland. I describe how the concept of Black masculinity I learned up until the fourth grade continued to influence my approach in middle school when I transferred from a Chicago Public School (CPS) to a suburban district. This chapter articulates how the relationship I had with my father and the influence of my friends shaped my performance as a Black male in a new environment. The goal of this chapter is to offer strategies for educators in suburban school districts that are interested in creating inclusive school cultures that can assist Black males to obtain authentic identity and higher academic achievement.

Chapter 4, *Follow the Leader*, discusses my evolving self-perception and the challenges I encountered with my teachers and school administration during my high school years. Through the narrative that explains how refusing to adhere to a school policy led to a suspension, I illustrate how I viewed myself as a teenager and how it influenced the choices I made to impress my friends and accumulate girlfriends. This chapter also reveals how a disturbing meeting with my school counselor after a suspension from school encouraged me to take a different academic approach. Throughout this chapter, I illustrate the value of programs that promote positive self-awareness and leadership among adolescent Black males, with the purpose to give alternative intervention options for professionals in high school settings.

In Chapter 5, *Undergrad and Underprepared*, I illustrate how my failures as an undergraduate student at the University of Illinois at Chicago led to later successes. This narrative begins with the challenges I encountered to get admitted to college and proceeds to discuss how poor decisions and study habits nearly jeopardized my undergraduate education. This chapter offers insight into preparing Black males for success in college, or other viable options post high school.

How can we encourage Black males to persevere through academic and other life challenges? Chapter 6, *From Pretty Boy to Man*, is about my experiences in graduate school and the problems I encountered while completing my dissertation. As a research assistant, I served as the lead graduate student on a four-year study investigating the experiences of Black males enrolled in a Chicago high school. The study explored how educators and administrators can make use of Black males' experiences to shape school culture and school policy. In this final chapter, I share the ordeal I endured to use the research for my dissertation. It discusses the perseverance I found to continue when accused of stealing research and the dream of earning a PhD became a nightmare. Chapter 6 illustrates how educators can foster the necessary internal motivation for Black males who possess aspirations for graduate and professional degrees.

In a Nutshell

Read the stories, take away the concepts, and apply them in your efforts to engage Black males in critical pedagogy. While the Black male experience is not universal, there are some commonalities that we share due to the invention and social implications of race and gender. The stories I present in this book are snapshots from my experiences and conversations I have had with other young Black males as a teacher, researcher, and mentor. It is through these moments of "real talk" that I have been able to offer practical advice as they attempt to make the most of their life and education choices.

The overarching goal of this book is to provide educators of Black males with information that can provide a gateway for meaningful relationships with their students. I wrote it in a format that can encourage students and educators to commit to life-long learning and improvement. As this book reveals, encounters with racism are an inevitable part of life for Black males in the United States. Too often many young men who are kissed by the sun and hugged by melanin at birth, are forced to succumb to structural inequalities and socially constructed identities. Educators of Black males have an opportunity to create safe spaces within schools and communities to allow for the voices of boys and men to be heard.

My work with the African Brazilian martial art of Capoeira has enabled me to facilitate many of the stories in this text that discuss my experiences with race, racism, and masculinity. When I lived in Chicago, I found Capoeira's dance, ritual, self-defense movements, and acrobatics to be a useful engagement tool for this work. Although Capoeira is not the focus of any of the chapters of this book, it would be careless not to mention its effectiveness as an activity for students at the middle, high school, and college levels of education. Practicing and sharing Capoeira is a passion of mine, and I continue to find use in it as part of my methods to inspire positivity among individuals and influence communities.

Although I currently live in Mexico, the image of Michael Brown's body is still with me. It serves as a harsh reminder of the structured nature of racism and the necessary work to change American society. I frequently contemplate how the education system underserved Michael Brown in broad daylight, while the criminal justice system waited in the shadows for his mistakes. Regardless of the inconsistent testimonies and other factors that led to a not guilty verdict in the case, evidence exists that Brown's decision to confront his limited choices in the land of opportunity, led to an unjustified murder. Unfortunately, there will be other Michael Browns who will lose their lives to racism and structured inequalities in a country that declares freedom for all and practices justice for some. With this awareness in mind and intention to encourage Black males to reach their potential, I share my story.

References

Cho, S., & Westley, R. (2002). Historicizing critical race theory's cutting edge: Key movements that performed the theory. In F. Valdes, M. J. Culp, & P. A. Harris (Eds.), *Crossroads directions, and a new critical race theory* (pp. 32–70). Philadelphia, PA: Temple University Press.

Corbado, D. W. (2011). Critical what? *Connecticut Law Review, 34*(5), 1595–1643.

Crenshaw, W. K. (1995). Mapping the margins: Intersectionality, identity politics, and violence against women of color. In W. K. Crenshaw, N. Gotanda, G. Peller, & K. Thomas (Eds.), *Critical race theory: The key writings that formed the movement* (pp. 357–383). New York, NY: The New Press.

Crenshaw, W. K. (2011). Twenty years of critical race theory: Looking back to move forward. *Connecticut Law Review, 43*(5), 1255–1346.

Delgado, R. (2000). Storytelling for oppositionists and others: A plea for narrative. In R. Delgado & J. Stefancic (Eds.), *Critical race theory: The cutting edge.*(pp. 64–74). Philadelphia, PA: Temple University Press.

Delgado, R., & Stefancic, J. (2000). *Critical race theory: The cutting edge.* Philadelphia, PA: Temple University Press.

Delgado, R., & Stefancic, J. (2001). *Critical race theory: An introduction.* New York, NY: New York University Press.

Harris, A. P. (2001). Foreword. In R. Delgado & J. Stefancic, J. (Eds.), *Critical race theory: An introduction* (pp. xvii–xxi). New York, NY: New York University Press.

Howard, T. C. (2014). *Black male (D): Peril and promise in the education of African American males.* New York, NY: Teachers College Press.

Ladson-Billings, G., & Tate, W. F. I. (2006). Toward a critical race theory of education. In A. D. Dixson & C. K. Rousseau (Eds.), *Critical race theory in education: All God's children got a song* (pp. 11–30). New York, NY: Routledge Taylor & Francis Group.

Parker, L., & Lynn, M. (2002). What's race got to do with it? Critical race theory's conflicts with and connections to qualitative research methodology and epistemology. *Qualitative Inquiry, 8*(1), 7–22.

Stovall, D. (2013). Fightin' the devil 24/7: Context, community, and critical race praxis in education. In Lynn, M. & Dixson, D. A. (Eds.), *Handbook of critical race theory in education* (pp. 289–301). New York, NY: Routledge.

Yosso, J. T. (2006). *Critical race counterstories along the Chicana/Chicano educational pipeline.* New York, NY: Routledge.

· 1 ·

BIRTH OF A PRETTY BOY

Introduction

I've been called Yellow Monkey, nigga, Black man, brother, father, son, king, God, pretty boy, and a host of other names, because of my gender, race, and long dreadlocks that currently touch my waist. Some of these terms have been used to convey love and respect, whereas others spilled from the lips of their speakers with intention full of hate and disrespect. Race and gender have undeniably influenced my life's experiences from the moment I was born a male, soon after socialized as a boy, and eventually matured into a Black man. I have presented myself to the world in response to the names others have called me and the internalization of their meanings.

Race is a social and historical construct based on perceived differences in human bodies. According to this definition, I am Black due to my physical features and a history of African ancestors enslaved in the United States. However, due to my lighter skin tone, I have often been the subject of many skin complexion-related jokes and frequently regarded as not quite "Black." My father is a Black man who was born in Madison, Wisconsin and my mother is a Black woman who was born and raised in Compton, California. By every measure of the definition of Blackness in US society, my family and I fit the bill.

Race is not a biological or scientific term, yet it influences social relationships, economic and educational opportunities. In Chicago, where I was born, it influenced the members of my community, the class of people I knew, and the schools I attended. Race is the product of a country that declared to hold values of freedom and liberty for all people, while simultaneously maintaining slavery.

Masculinity is the performance of behaviors we have come to accept as normal for males. It is how males learn to be boys. Masculinity taught me boys: fight, climb trees, work hard, like girls, get dirty, play sports and engage in other gender specific performances. It is through the lenses of race and masculinity I learned how to be a Black man and survive in Chicago and the surrounding south suburbs.

In the 1980s researchers began to put an increased focus on the experiences of Black males in education settings (Fultz & Brown, 2008; Garibaldi, 2007); this was the same time I began school. I was among the Black males referred to as, "a dying population," "in crisis," "an endangered species," "at risk," and "misdiagnosed" in the prominent research of this era (Bailey, 1983; Fultz & Brown, 2008; Gibbs, 1988; Leavy, 1983; Parham & McDavis, 1987; Porter, 1997, Strickland, 1989; Young, 2004). Such beliefs and concerns about my life in Chicago influenced my parents' decision to move my family from the city to the south suburbs.

Growing up as a young Black man, who others called Yellow, in Chicago and a south suburb called South Holland, I became aware of the intersections between race, masculinity, and my identity. I was always conscious of the reality that, by society's standards, I was racially classified as Black. Play fighting, participating in sports activities, climbing trees were all things I enjoyed and subscribed to as a boy. Clearly, I was a Black boy, but my family members and friends often teased me due to my lighter skin, long eyelashes, small stature, hair texture, and a natural gift to find trouble. Frequently, people called me a pretty boy and Yellow, because of my facial features.

My goal for this chapter is to share what I learned from my home environment and early school experiences about what it means to be a Black boy in America. I discuss my relationship with my dad and the approach to masculinity he passed to me from his father. This opening narrative begins with my family, not because I believe the families of Black male students are the sole culprits to blame for failures or praise for successes. However, it is imperative we consider the family as the foundation for the lives of Black boys and men.

Families of color are not independent units exempt from the impact of structured inequalities. If we desire to significantly improve the lives of Black males and increase their potential for positive contributions to society, we must understand their familial backgrounds and also work to disrupt systemic racism within the education, judicial, and healthcare systems. At the end of this chapter, you should be able to understand the self-perception I internalized from a young age and how some Black males will begin school with firm, limiting beliefs about their potential influenced by race, gender and the expectations of masculinity performances.

Birth of a Pretty Boy

"Mom, I think she is a racist. I didn't do anything this time." "What makes you think she is a racist? Do you know what a racist is?" "I mean, I feel like she picks on my friends and me. I'm not sure why." This exchange was part of a conversation I had with my mother in the third grade after the school's assistant principal decided to call home and request a family conference.

Earlier that day, one of my classmates called me a White pretty boy, and I was fed up. I was tired of defending that I was Black and so I decided to punch him in the face. I believed Black males were strong and so to prove I was not weak, I decided to fight. One of my teachers saw me throw the first punch that turned into a brawl, so she sent me to Assistant Principal Ms. Newark's, office. Because of my frequent behavioral related infractions, Ms. Newark knew me too well.

I often felt Ms. Newark's eyes on me as I walked throughout the school building. There was more than one occasion when she decided to call me out of the line with my classmates to make threats in the event I decided to misbehave. Yes, I frequently acted out in school but there were also many situations when I was following orders and threatened with consequences. From an early age I saw school as less of a place for education and more as an institution designed to instill order and control.

At home, I was the only boy with five sisters, and because of our differences in approaches to school and other mannerisms, I frequently wondered if the hospital switched me at birth. It didn't help that my sisters used to encourage an adoption theory as evidence of the fact I was the only boy among five girls. I used to ask my mother if I had a different father and she would always respond with a soft laugh and a firm "no." My mother had vivid memories of the day I was born and the day my father hoped I was born.

Mom told me when she gave birth to my sister Erica, the first words from my father's mouth were, "Oh ... another girl." Erica was the fourth girl in a row born to my parents, and it was clear while my dad was happy to be a father again, he was wishing and praying for a boy. Reminding her at the hospital right after she had given birth was just not the best time to make this known.

My mother carried Erica for nine months, while also taking care of the other three small children who were very close in age. Traveling was nearly an every other weekend occurrence for my father who was a rising church pastor during these early years. He often left my mother alone or with a member of the church while he attended affairs related to his life's calling. During the birth of Erica, my mom experienced a grueling time-intensive labor, and afterward wanted nothing more than to rest and receive positive recognition for another life she brought into the world. However, somewhere between the home and the hospital, my father's comments, "Oh, another girl," indicated he lost his mind!

My dad didn't think much of his response to Erica's birth because he learned men are direct and say what is on their mind. My mother would never admit this, but it is feasible to suggest immediately following the birth of her fourth consecutive child, she did not feel valued and appreciated. She loved my father and was angry with him for not deciding to express gratitude for a beautiful baby girl. The baby's sex was irrelevant to my mother, but my father desperately wanted a male.

Nearly two years after Erica, my father's prayers and wishes were answered. I was born to Emery and Pearl at Mercy Hospital in Chicago on a cold, snowy, and windy November day. My mother told me my dad was extremely excited. He was finally able to pass down the family name and begin instilling the values in me he learned from his father.

It seemed like a natural fit for my father to name me after his dad who he held in great admiration and respect. My mother wanted to give me the name Corey but my father was determined to honor his father. Vernon Corey was the compromise they agreed upon, and the legacy of my grandfather's name continued through me.

To live up to my grandfather's legacy, I would have to carry myself with dignity, pride, and a desire to work hard. My grandfather emphasized the importance of education and hard work. If my grandfather were alive on the day I revisited the assistant principal's office, he would have been disappointed. My father told me my grandfather taught him to value school and to demonstrate respect for his peers and especially other adults.

Although my grandfather experienced a premature death, his influence remained with my dad. He is extremely self-disciplined, kind, full of integrity, and a hard worker. From what I was told, my dad's father was also a great man who was a strict disciplinarian and willing to do whatever it took to provide for his family. I can only believe the stories passed down to me because I never had the chance to meet my grandfather. While working as a landscaper for his family's tree cutting business, my grandfather fell from a tree and died before I was born. When my grandfather passed away, my father committed himself to raise a son based on the virtues and ideas his dad instilled in him.

My father picked me up from school early on that day Assistant Principal Newark called home. I usually walked home, so I knew at the sight of my father's car, I was in trouble. After he scolded me for the phone call he received that interrupted his study time, he said five words no child likes to hear from their parents, "just wait until we get home." I knew punishment was imminent, so I tried to make conversation with an intention to convince him to forget.

While riding in the car with my dad home, I tried to explain to him the reasons for my actions and how I felt as a Black boy who others called Yellow. My classmates, neighborhood friends, sisters, and others frequently made the color of my skin the subject of their jokes. As Haki Madhubuti (2006), who also grew up as a Black boy with lighter skin, confirms in his memoir, too often Black males with lighter skin are chastised for "not being Black enough" due to skin color and hair texture. I frequently wrestled with the idea of "not being Black enough," and consistently tried to prove myself.

As a confused Black boy and my parents' only son, I often looked to my father for validation. On the ride home from school that turned into a pit stop at the church my father pastored, I decided to use the extra time in the car to conjure up some sympathy. Our talk began with an innocent observation, followed by a question. "Dad, I am Black. Why do I have blonde hair on my arm?" "Well somewhere down the line, we have family that is White." "Really? You and mom are not White." "Yes." His one-word response told me I was not getting anywhere in that conversation, so I changed the topic and asked about my grandfather.

My grandfather lived by the code that children were to be seen and rarely heard. This idea means merely that children make a household complete, but they need to understand their place and remain respectful to their elders. My grandfather ensured my father and his siblings listened to all adults by establishing a household with firm rules and severe consequences for any violators. Discipline, working hard, and displaying a minimum of emotions were critical to my grandfather's beliefs about masculinity. My father is a man very similar to how I imagine my grandfather.

I asked my father if he ever got in trouble during school and how his dad handled the situation. He responded, "My father made it clear that if an adult spoke to you, it was mandatory that you respond right away." I followed-up and asked what the consequences were if you did not reply to an adult immediately. Without hesitation, my father said, "The famous beat down." As the four words, "the famous beat down," escaped his mouth, I moved as close to the passenger door as possible.

In education, my father expected me as a Black boy and his only son to live up to his mantra: "Be the labor great or small do it well or not at all." My dad used to repeat his mantra whenever my siblings, or I participated in any task. He lived by these words and used a fine needle to sew it into our brains. It did not matter if we were sweeping the floor, working on a homework assignment, or playing a sport, if my father were near we would hear his mantra as a means to encourage us to do our best. School was not an exception to this rule, and as I probed to get more from him in regards to his upbringing, I learned he gathered this perspective from his parents' example of hard work and discipline.

Vernon Denis Lindsay, my grandfather, believed in the necessity of a whooping to ensure his children put forth their best effort and behavior at school or elsewhere. A whooping is different from a spanking, and it is not a whipping. In my household, a whooping involved a leather belt called "the brown bruiser," and it was used to hit my siblings and me on our butts, legs, or hands. The use of "the brown bruiser," was inherited from my father's parents who put their faith in God and the whooping to correct inappropriate behavior and academic underachievement.

Like me, my father was the only son of my grandparents. His status as the only one undeniably influenced a special relationship with his mom and dad. When I asked him to give more details about how his father established discipline in the house, he replied, "my sisters can really recall this trauma of our childhood, but I like to forget about it." That was his code language for indicating that his sisters were whooped more than him. His privilege as the only boy enabled him to "forget about it." When I got in trouble in the third grade, and the assistant principal called home, I was hoping that my status as the only boy would also produce a lenient punishment.

As mentioned above, we didn't go directly home from school, but to the church he pastored. On the drive, he continued to talk about his father and what he taught him about manhood. My grandfather co-owned a landscaping company, served as a deacon in his church, and took great pride in working hard to meet the financial needs of his family. One of my father's first employment positions was working with his uncles in the family business. It was during various jobs cutting down trees for residential and corporate clients my dad witnessed the amount of effort it took for his father to provide for his family.

At the local church, my father also saw his dad serve as one of the spiritual leaders of the congregation. My grandfather was a deacon, so nearly every Sunday my dad and his siblings attended the weekly service. Through assisting the pastor and members of the congregation, serving as a leader at home, and working in the landscaping industry, my grandfather embodied a version of masculinity equitable with hard work, perseverance, sacrifice, and discipline. This message of manhood is what my father accepted as the truth and instilled in me as a child.

As a child, I wanted to mirror my father's every footstep. I followed him around the house, spent time with him at the church, and mimicked his Sunday sermons at home. Of all the time I spent with my dad, tears never fell from his eyes. He was always a man of few words and limited emotions. The exception to his frequently reserved demeanor was only at church during his sermons in the pulpit.

For many years, I saw crying as a divine gift accessed by women, girls, and pastors like my dad. My father's spiritual tears consistently appeared in a story about his grandmother. He began the story with the explanation of how she brought him to church and then transitioned to his crying moment where he explained his grandmother's strong faith in Jesus. I didn't know what to make of it as a child, but I knew that outside of the pulpit, boys did not cry.

Throughout many of my early years, hyper masculine depictions of Black male identity had a strong influence on how I perceived myself. Although I admired my father, his occupation as a pastor did not have the same lure as the lifestyles I believed professional athletes, rappers, actors, and others enjoyed. I wanted to be recognized as tough by my peers. If I felt threatened, I refused to back down and a fight often ensued. I accepted a negative version of my identity, because I was unable to see how my gender and race were socially scripted.

A part of the reason why I got in trouble in the third grade, was because I believed certain behaviors were not acceptable for Black boys. As the only boy in my family, I needed to show a minimum of emotions and fight others to prove I was "all-boy." My sisters were the epitome of the social construction of femininity; they took pride in their physical appearances, cried when hurt, were often soft-spoken, and for the most part well-mannered. People frequently said I looked like I wore mascara because my eyelashes were long; my fade haircut, style of clothing, and disruptive behavior served as my saving grace.

My father's example taught me Black boys must follow their passions in life and stay disciplined. He started preaching at age 18 as a youth pastor, and when I was in the third grade, he was the lead pastor of a church with 500 members. For over twenty years, he exemplified the importance of following your passion and remaining committed to the journey. With the relentless love and support of my mom, my dad led our household and was an excellent provider for my family.

For most of my childhood, our family's needs were met with one income and the assistance of the church. We did not have a lavish lifestyle full of luxuries, but we did have food, clothing, and shelter. My parents took advantage of government assisted food services such as Women Infants and Children (WIC) and on multiple occasions, I had to wear the latest pair of XJ 900 tennis shoes instead of the Air Jordan's which were extremely popular among my friends. Although I was unable to have some of the luxury items I desired as a child, the church ensured our family had the necessities.

As a senior pastor and leader of the Holiness denomination, my father frequently traveled for church-related affairs. His schedule did not allow my mother to hold a job outside of the home, so for many years, she was a full-time homemaker. Although it was not a progressive family structure, this arrangement worked for them. Frequently, my mother likes to remind me of the challenges she had with raising six children.

Whenever a teacher or in this case an administrator called home, I desperately hoped that my mother would take my position on the problem. I had this vision of my mother going with me to school and cussing out the school staff in defense of my behavior. However, nothing could be more contrary to my mother's personality. She often sang gospel hymns around the house as she completed chores, baked sweets for our neighbors, and rarely raised her voice at me and my sisters. The chances of my mother cussing out a member of the school staff were extremely limited, despite my mother's upbringing in one of the notorious neighborhoods of Los Angeles.

As one of thirteen children raised in a two bedroom, one bathroom home in Compton, California, my mother knew sacrifice. Her father was a plasterer by trade and did not make nearly enough money to cover all the living expenses for his family. He was also an alcoholic and abusive toward my grandmother, which put an additional strain on the family's resources and quality of life. When my mom took an interest in singing and playing the piano, my grandmother began to offer ironing services to cover the $2 expense for weekly music lessons. From an early age, living with less outlined my mother's story.

In college, my mom majored in music education with the goal to pursue a career as an opera singer. She attended college on a music scholarship. When I asked her about the impact of the music lessons on her talent, she told me her father went from telling her to "shut that racket" when she sang around the house to declaring "child you have a million dollar voice." She was dedicated to her craft and self-disciplined when it came to making time to practice. My mother had the potential to be a successful opera singer and decided not to pursue her dream to focus on the future of her family.

There were many moments when I am sure my home tested my mother's sanity. My father was frequently away traveling and handling affairs related to the church, which left my mother alone with six kids to manage. When my sisters and I got into fights, my mother was the one who resolved many of the conflicts. I distinctly remember the reprimand that: "Boys don't hit girls." On the occasions, I did allow my anger to get the best of me, and I hit one of my sisters, the punishment was severe. My mom along with my father taught me from a young age Black boys are not abusive toward women.

In the third grade when Ms. Newark called home, I expected to see the "brown bruiser" waiting for me in my father's home office. After stopping by the church for approximately an hour so my father could finish up some work, we drove to the house in what felt like record time. As we pulled up and my dad put the car in park, my heart began to race. I remembered his earlier threat when he picked me up from school, "wait until we get home," and I knew that was code for his inherited version of his father's "famous beat down."

We exited the car and walked together, up the partially paved driveway of our home located on 83rd and Calumet on Chicago's Southside. As soon as we opened the door, I tapped into some divine and misconceived feminine energy to cry, because I did not want a whooping. My parents were not abusive, but they were supporters of the Bible verse that says spare the rod and spoil the child when my sisters and I did not behave to the level of their expectations.

The first words my dad told me after closing the front door behind him was, "Vernon, go to my office." I cried harder because I knew the inevitable result of a private meeting in his office. In this bedroom, located on the first floor of our home was his study, where he stored hundreds of books about Christianity and leadership. The walls were lined with wooden bookcases filled with resources he used for his sermons and leisure time study. It was his oasis of refuge and meditation; I saw it as the room where conviction and sentencing occurred.

I walked into my dad's office and saw my mother sitting at the desk. Before they could start, I sat on the floor and began to cry. Oh no, I thought "they are going to do a tag team on me with the brown bruiser." I cried harder. My mother said, "Vernon, please calm down we are not going to give you a whooping." I continued to cry because I knew getting in trouble in school was not acceptable and if it wasn't a whooping some other more severe form of punishment, like no cartoons for a month was coming my way. My mother calmly quelled my fears and said that we are going to talk.

That's when I blurted, "I think the Assistant Principal Newark is a racist." My mom was surprised at what I said and asked me to repeat myself. I told her I didn't know exactly what being a racist meant, but that I believed she picked on me and my friends because we were Black boys. Assistant Principal Newark was White and one of the few White staff members at my elementary school. My mother listened and didn't immediately respond. When she did, it was with my punishment.

I was not allowed to watch television or hang out with my friends because I got in trouble at school. There would be no cartoons or time outside to play sports, tag or ride bikes. These restrictions were worse than a whooping, because they lasted more than a couple of minutes. I didn't know if my punishment was going to last two weeks or two years. I was told merely no cartoons or time to hang out with my friends.

My boys were my life as a child. They were a significant influence on how I came to learn about my roles in life. The lessons we shared did not take place inside of a formal classroom but in the vacant lots, playgrounds, and backyards where we played pickup games of basketball, football, and baseball. These lessons continued after the games in basements and bedrooms, where I learned how to fight and play video games. They taught me about competition, and how to defend myself. I taught them the safest way to fall, and how to get back up without crying.

My parents talked at me for about an hour to get a truthful version of what happened at school. I knew being called a White pretty boy was not a good reason to fight, so I just listened to them explain why it was so important that I did well in school. Near the end of our conversation where I listened, and they talked, there was an effort to encourage me.

They told me I was smart, a natural leader among my friends, and had the potential to do great things with my life. A phone call home from an administrator or teacher was unacceptable for someone with my abilities and characteristics. My father said, "your genuine friends will always be there, and you do not need to act out in school to gain their attention and respect." According to my parents, I possessed everything I needed to be successful in life. As they continued to scold and encourage me, I could hear my sisters laughing on the other side of the door.

During what appeared to be the longest talk of my life, my parents had to stop more than once to tell my sisters to find some of their business. They were waiting in the hallway, listening to our conversation, and laughing every time I tried to explain. When my parents stopped and opened the door, they would scream, run, and then apologize. Five-ten minutes later they resumed their positions on the other side of my father's office door. They waited in anticipation of the brown bruiser and wanted to hear me cry.

When I left my father's study, the first thing Erica said to me was, "Look at the Yellow Monkey who got in trouble at school again." My other four sisters started to laugh. I was angry and wanted to punch Erica like I did the kid in school, but I remembered my mother telling me that "boys don't hit girls." Hitting my sisters was a cardinal sin in my household, and I was already in trouble. So instead of hitting Erica, I did the second best thing I could, I said "shut-up Yellow Dracula!"

Like many people who are born in societies and impacted by the fallacies of race, my sisters and I internalized and reinforced our oppression from a young age. We placed value on ourselves based on the perceived flaws in our physical appearances. My sisters teased me due to my skin color, height, and other physical features. I reciprocated name-calling and teasing because I didn't love myself or understand my history as a person of African descent.

We were unaware of the Willie Lynch doctrine that informed practices on slave plantations. It divided people based on skin color, gender, and age to control and maintain order. Such ideas that people with lighter skin are somehow inherently better than people with darker skin is a derivative of the Willie Lynch philosophies. As a young Black boy, I didn't understand how the negative perceptions I internalized of myself and held of others were part of a broader and dark history.

Camile and Melanie are my oldest sisters who have blossomed into beautiful, intelligent women. However, when we were children, they were not exempt from insults. My eldest sister Camile was the heaviest among us, and so we replaced her given name with "Fatty." Melanie was chastised for having darker skin, and so we called her "Blackie." My sisters and I didn't understand the reason why we called Melanie "Blackie" was because we had like others, unfortunately, believed that having dark skin was bad and unattractive. Despite coming from a home that taught us to respect all persons regardless of their complexion, it was evident we adopted other beliefs about our bodies. My house reflected the social implications of race and the notion of colorism.

Colorism, the practice of differential treatment based on skin tone variations within the Black community, is a byproduct of the mentioned above Willie Lynch doctrine. In a contemporary context Black people with lighter skin are viewed as more attractive and in some cases offered more opportunities for economic and social mobility. These opportunities that were also part of my childhood are based on ideologies in alignment with notions of racism (White supremacy), which declare that people with lighter skin possess more value within society. Colorism also supports misperceptions of Black people with darker skin as less attractive, unintelligent, and therefore justified in occupying lower socioeconomic positions.

We didn't understand the implications of our words as children, and so we ostracized each other based on physical characteristics. My third sister after Melanie was Rachel, and we called her "Musty" due to how we perceived her body odor. We would say things to Rachel such as, "You smell like you've been holding onions in a headlock. Go take a bath." Erica, my fourth sister in line, was called "Dracula", because her two front teeth resembled fangs like the character who appears in films and books. My youngest sister Brittany had long, thick, and kinky hair. Due to her hair texture we called nappy, she was gifted with the name "Napola". As children, we didn't quite understand how race influenced our perceptions of beauty and self-worth.

I received the name "Yellow Monkey", due to my fair skin complexion, the size of my ears, my short height, and the behaviors I adopted as the only boy in the family. My sisters said I looked like a monkey because I had big ears that stuck out from the sides of my head. I've always had relatively light skin when compared with other Black people, therefore my sisters were the first, but not the last, to declare Yellow Monkey as a suitable substitute for Vernon. In my efforts to live up to the expectations of boys' behavior, I also managed to get into a lot of trouble as a child which supported this unwelcomed nickname.

When I left my father's office after being scolded for misbehaving in school, my sister Erica smiled at me like the Cheshire cat from *Alice in Wonderland* and called me Yellow Monkey. I had to return the favor and tease her with the name I knew that she despised, Dracula. We went back and forth for a few seconds until my mother stopped it and told me to go to my bedroom. I knew I had already been spared once from the "brown bruiser" so I didn't push back and went directly to the bedroom I shared with my youngest sister, Brittany. The time alone gave me time to prepare myself for the conference with Assistant Principal Newark scheduled for the next morning.

How could I explain to my parents and the woman who I was convinced was a card-carrying racist, Ms. Newark, the conflict that I was having at school? In my early years, I approached school with multiple messages about me and my potential. My sisters called me Yellow Monkey, because of my physical features and animalistic, but socially deemed appropriate boy behavior. I had parents who told me I was smart, attractive and a natural leader among my friends. Music, television and other forms of media were telling me to emulate professional athletes and criminals. My friends teased me by calling me names such as high Yellow and pretty boy, but I knew I was Black.

When it came to school, I didn't know myself or my potential as a young Black boy from Chicago's Southside. I frequently ignored the positive compliments and held on to everything negative said about me and the opportunities for my life. This practice of accepting what others thought of me sharpened my physical skills as a fighter and fueled limiting beliefs that school could not improve the opportunities for me in life. Negative internalized beliefs about my potential as a Black boy, coupled with my perception of an irrelevant school curriculum, created a need to live up to the expectations of others.

At school, I went to extreme efforts to gain friends and recognition as one of the cool kids. There were seasons when my parents received weekly requests for parent-teacher conferences because I was disruptive in class and had fist fights with my peers. I knew I was smart and capable of doing well in any academic subject, but I downplayed my intelligence for fear of being recognized as a nerd. Despite my parent's efforts to help me develop a positive sense of self, I adopted the wrong messages about my identity as a Black male and saw school as the stage to perform the character I wanted to embody.

When I arrived at the school with my mom on the day after the assistant principal called home in the third grade, I was afraid. I was concerned my mom might change her mind and return to thinking a whooping was the solution for my misbehavior in school. As we entered the school's office and sat in the lobby's chairs for what felt like a lifetime, my heart beat faster every minute in anticipation of what Ms. Newark would say about my behavior.

Eventually, Assistant Principal Newark came out and greeted my mom. She said hello to me also, but I ignored her. After sitting and listening for about fifteen minutes of her rendition of the story, my mother responded and said, "Vernon thinks you're a racist." Ms. Newark's face turned red and made a look that conveyed she was uncomfortable. Then she responded, "That's funny. I can't be a racist. I have Black friends."

I couldn't articulate it at the time, but her response just seemed a tad odd to me. In my mother's reply that included a condescending laugh followed by silence, I knew that something was not right. A person who has friends of color can also have the potential to participate in and practice racism. Racism is individual and systemic practices of discriminatory treatment toward others based on perceived differences in physical features.

As a Black male who internalized limiting beliefs about his race and gender, it was a challenge to decipher between internal and external oppression. I must acknowledge the decisions I made to fight my peers and disrupt my teacher's lesson plans. It is also important to consider the source of the messages that I believed and convinced me of self-destructive behavioral choices. At home and among my friends there was a fabricated expectation of masculinity that I attempted to use as a measure of my self-worth. In my school, I didn't see a connection between the curriculum and preparation for achievements later in life. While my father was active in my life, I remained influenced by the dominant images that undermined the potential of Black males.

The constructs of race and gender coupled with masculinity influenced my educational experiences. Either my parents were too tired to give me a whooping on that day in the third grade, or they took pity on me when they realized that my school experiences would be different from my sisters. A challenge of growing up as a Black male or another person of color in America is that it is not always clear whether you are being treated poorly due to race, gender or some other reason. However, for me and others, there was and remains a consistent feeling of not belonging and or being offered the same opportunities as people who are identified as White. The overt signs of racism such as "for colored only" have been removed, but many of the practices persist in individuals and are embedded within the structures of the United States. It would be many years before I could really make sense of my experiences in the third grade, but a trip to Florida during spring break of fourth grade pushed me in the right path toward an answer to understanding the implications of my identity as a Black boy.

How can we use this story to understand more about the experiences of some Black males in school as they navigate race and masculinity?

Racial identity and notions of masculinity influence academic achievement among Black males. Race is a political, invented, and social historical concept codified by law and validated via cultural and material economies (Gotanda, 1991; Haney Lopez, 1996; Harris, 1995; Omi & Winant, 1994; Roberts, 2011; Vaught, 2011; Winant, 2001). Masculinity is the social and cultural construction of what it means to be a man, which includes the performance of mutually accepted behaviors of dress style, disposition, and attitude by society (Brod & Kaufman, 1994; Davis, 2006; Noguera, 2001). When Black males are unable to embrace healthy visions of themselves, their academic performance in school suffers.

As indicated in the story, my first teachers of race and masculinity were from my family, school, and environment. They informed me of the acceptable behaviors for Black boys born in the United States. On the one hand, my father taught me to have a strong work ethic, practice self-discipline, and to be well mannered; whereas in school I was convinced fighting and underperforming in school were the measures of Black male identity. I grew up with beliefs that boys do not cry, because my father didn't show emotion out of the pulpit where he preached his Sunday sermons. For me, very few things were worse than being teased for my light skin complexion or being called a girl like my sisters. The constructs of race and masculinity embraced at home and in my community spilled into my behavior in school.

I learned Black masculinity was equated with violence and so to prove I could meet the mark I fought my peers. Ferguson (2000) noted that the criminalization of young Black males is related to the performance of Black masculinity that impedes academic achievement in public schools. In the schools I attended, I frequently resorted to violence to live up to the performance standards of Black masculinity. These choices led to encounters with the assistant principal as illustrated in this chapter. I experienced what Davis (2006) suggests as a need among Black males to define masculinity through a normative lens that emphasizes racial awareness through the context of oppression and poor academic achievement.

Similar to me, some Black males will enter schools confused about their identity, and convinced that displays of their physical strength coupled with underperforming in academics are essential to earning respect. They will need teachers and others who can serve as reliable positive mentors to foster positive notions about Black male identity. Without the proper support tools, schools will continue to be a place to perform and release frustration with pervasive negative indications of what it means to be Black and male. It is vital that schools invest in the creation of safe spaces for meaningful dialogue and analysis, between youth and adults.

Allowing for opportunities to express vulnerability is especially crucial for Black males who can enter schools convinced violence or overt displays of their physical strength are the best routes to prove their value. Despite my father's presence and persistence to teach me discipline, hard work, and respect, I turned to fighting to resolve conflicts. I immediately decided to punch my classmate when he called me a White pretty boy because I believed a passive response would not garnish the admiration I desperately wanted to receive from my peers. In the third grade, I had no idea many of the negative beliefs that I accepted about myself and my friends were invented and derived from environments outside of my community. In the fourth grade, the vision of myself began to shift after a spring break trip to Florida.

To download the FREE PDF discussion guide, please visit: www.vlindsayphd .com/crtblackmales

References

Bailey, P. (1983, August). A manchild of the 80s: Boys meet the challenge of growing up in Harlem. *USA Ebony*, pp. 68–72.

Brod, H., & Kaufman, M. (Eds.). (1994). *Theorizing masculinities*. Thousand Oaks, CA: Sage.

Davis, J. E. (2006). Research at the margin: Mapping masculinity and mobility of African-American high school dropouts. *International Journal of Qualitative Studies in Education, 19*(3), 289–305.

Ferguson, A. A. (2000). *Bad boys: Public schools in the making of black masculinity*. Ann Arbor, MI: University of Michigan Press.

Fultz, M., & Brown, A. (2008). Historical perspectives on African American males as subjects of education policy. *American Behavioral Scientist, 51*(7), 854–871.

Garibaldi, M. A. (2007). The educational status of African American males in the 21st century. *Journal of Negro Education, 76*(3), 324–333.

Gibbs, J. T. (1988). *Young, black and male in America: An endangered species*. New York, NY: Auburn House.

Gotanda, N. (1991). A critique of "our constitution is color-blind." *Stanford Law Review, 44*, 1–69.

Haney Lopez, I. F. (1996). *White by law: The legal construction of race*. New York, NY: New York University Press.

Harris, C. I. (1995). Whiteness as property. In K. Crenshaw, N. Gotanda, & K. Thomas (Eds.), *Critical race theory: The key writings that formed the movement* (pp. 276–291). New York, NY: New Press.

Leavy, W. (1983, August). Is the Black male an endangered species? *Ebony*, pp. 41–46.

Madhubuti, H. R. (2006). *Yellow Black: The first twenty-one years of a poet's life*. Chicago, IL: Third World Press.

Noguera, P. (2001, December 1). Joaquin's dilemma: Understanding the link between racial identity and school-related behaviors. *Motion Magazine*. Retrieved March 12, 2013, from http://www.inmotionmagazine.com/er/pnjoaqref.html

Omi, M., & Winant, H. (1994). *Racial formation in the United States: From the 1960s to the 1990s*. New York, NY: Routledge.

Parham, T., & McDavis, R. (1987). Black men, an endangered species: Who's really pulling the trigger? *Journal of Counseling and Development, 66*, 24–27.

Porter, M. (1997). *Kill them before they grow: Misdiagnosis of African American boys in American classrooms*. Chicago, IL: African American Images.

Roberts, D. (2011). *Fatal invention: How science, politics, and big business re-create race in the twenty-first century*. New York, NY: The New Press.

Strickland, W. (1989, November). Our men in crisis: Together we must meet the enormous challenge facing Black men. *Essence*, pp. 49–52.

Vaught, E. S. (2011). *Racism, public schooling and the entrenchment of white supremacy: A critical race ethnography*. Albany, NY: State University of New York Press.

Winant, H. (2001). *The world is a ghetto: Race and democracy since World War II*. New York, NY: Basic Books.

Young, A. A. (2004). *The minds of marginalized Black men: Making sense of mobility, opportunity and future life chances*. Princeton, NJ: Princeton University Press.

· 2 ·

THE GIRL IN THE PINK BIKINI

Introduction

In the fourth grade, my family continued to live in Chatham, a racially segregated community on Chicago's Southside. The overwhelming majority of
my neighbors, friends, and classmates were Black. My father also continued
to pastor a church in the Roseland community where a significant portion of
the residents identified as Black or African-American. Until the fourth grade,
I thought of myself through the lenses of people who looked like me and were
part of my community.

Spring break during my fourth-grade year in school was the first time. It
was the first time that I can remember spending time with people who are
identified as White, or as Coates (2015) defines "Americans who believe they
are White," and feeling inferior due to the color of my skin. There were no
White families who lived in my Chicago neighborhood. However, a spring
break trip to Florida introduced me to a White girl and boy who exposed me to
a different perspective of my identity as a Black boy from Chicago's Southside.

Racism is individual beliefs and systemic actions that support subjugation
based on perceived differences in human bodies; this includes the ideas and
actions that become policies and laws supporting a range of social inequalities.

It is supported by people and permeates structures of the education, health-care, criminal justice, and a host of other related systems. Racism is not always overt, but rather it is an intricate relationship supported by influential individuals who are invested in maintaining the unequal distribution of resources. In the fourth grade, I had my first experiences with White children who held beliefs consistent with racism.

Racism impacts the lives of Black male students. One indicator is the proliferation of videos available via social media and television that show police officers killing Black males without any legal repercussions. A 2015 study indicated Black males between the ages of 15–34 are nine times more likely to be murdered by the police than any other group of American people (Swaine, Laughland, Lartey, & McCarthy, 2015). In 2012 only 59% of Black males enrolled in high schools earned a diploma (Holzman, 2012). To provide evidence of the systems that support homicide in particular and racial inequalities in general, it is imperative to examine the beliefs that inform some Americans who believe they are White.

In the narrative that follows, I explore my first lesson in how some individuals outside of my community viewed me as a Black male. Within the literature of critical race theory, counter narratives are an important tool to understand how inequalities persist within the education system (Delgado, 2000; Yosso, 2006). In working with Black males, I have found that engaging self-reflection to create positive self-awareness is critical to unlocking academic potential. A segue to having conversations about experiences with racism can be difficult; one method to begin the discussion is to ask students about their dreams. From this starting point of sharing aspirations and narratives, we can begin to analyze the impact of racism and present methods that can encourage positive thoughts and actions.

The Girl in the Pink Bikini

During my elementary years of education, I remember a reoccurring dream of a school takeover. I dreamed that together with my classmates we engaged in protest and resistance to replace the teachers and administrators. We wanted to escape the boredom of our classrooms and make school our playground. I don't remember any vivid details of how we succeeded, but I can say that the takeover was not violent. This dream was reflective of the disconnect I felt between my life, a school culture that emphasized control, and curricula I believed would not position me for future achievements. Like many youth, I did not enjoy school and looked forward to every holiday.

It was about two months before spring break when my mother received a call from my Aunt Mignon, who offered to take me on vacation to Florida with my cousin Stevie. Any time spent with my cousin was appreciated because I was the only boy living in a home with five girls. While I had plenty of male friends in my neighborhood, there was an inevitable time of departure that I dreaded after each opportunity together. Seven days of uninterrupted time to hang out with my cousin who was close to my age sounded like paradise. I could barely contain myself in anticipation of my father's return home, to get an answer on whether or not I would be able to attend the trip.

Though my father eventually allowed me to go on the trip, he was not without reservations: specifically, the financial burden this trip would take on my family was of major concern. Mignon ran a successful salon and her husband, Bruce, was a pediatrician. They lived in an amazing home with a pink façade on the street called Longwood in Chicago's exclusive Beverley neighborhood. I remember their leather couches and the glass display cases in their family room full of Sports Illustrated VHS tapes. As a huge Chicago Bulls fan, it was great to spend time in their home and watch episodes of the documentaries on Jordan and the Bulls. I enjoyed visiting my cousin's house, because he lived with things my family of eight did not have on a ministerial salary. As far as my father was concerned, the trip to Florida was a luxury and not a necessity. Thankfully, my mother saw it beyond the price tag and as an opportunity for me to experience something special with my cousin.

I was excited when my aunt and uncle asked my parents if it would be ok for me to join them on their family trip to Florida. By the fourth grade I had some experience traveling with my family to attend church-related activities, but up until this point, I had never been to Florida. I always wanted to go to Disney World and Universal Studios, but my family could not afford the trip. My parents would have had to pay for eight airline tickets, eight theme park admissions, and hotel accommodations for eight people, along with the additional expenses of food and shopping. We just did not have that kind of extra money laying around the house. My father reminded me of this several times before he reluctantly allowed me to go.

My expectations for the trip to Florida were high because I knew it was a unique opportunity unavailable to my sisters. When we arrived in Orlando, we rented a car at the airport and drove to my aunt and uncle's timeshare located within a gated community. Every home in this neighborhood had a similar architectural design: they were two stories with brown Spanish tile roofs, beige painted exteriors, and two car garages. Each home was surrounded with green grass, a colorful array of flowers, and palm trees that reached over thirty feet into the sky. It was apparent that I was far away from my home on the Southside of Chicago.

One of the first activities my cousin and I wanted to do was visit the community swimming pool advertised in the timeshare brochure. We liked to swim, and believed it would also be the place where we would have the opportunity to meet other children our age. According to the brochure, the pool was located in the center of the timeshare complex in the residential entertainment corridor. This central location inside of the gated community provided access to a state-of-the-art video game arcade, a gift shop, a five-star restaurant, and an indoor lagoon with a swimming pool equipped with a diving board and waterslide. As far as Stevie and I were concerned, this was the best starting point for our Florida adventure.

My aunt and uncle had a different set of plans and wanted us to eat before setting out to discover our new surroundings. They were in charge, so we had no choice but to comply with their wishes and join them at the restaurant. However, Stevie and I did not lose sight of our desire to check out the space that we were blessed to call home for the next five days. After we placed our order with the waiter, we asked Aunt Mignon and Uncle Bruce if it would be possible to take a solo trip down the hall to the pool. They hesitantly agreed under two conditions. First, we were forbidden to set foot in the pool; second, we had to return to the table within fifteen minutes. These instructions came with the threat they would call our names over the intercom system if we did not return in time, which was motivation enough to locate the pool and get back to the table as quick as possible. The idea of hearing our names over the intercom system and, more importantly, being embarrassed in front of other kids was not something we wanted to experience. Other children were walking around, and we did not want to earn the reputation of babies who lost mommy and daddy.

The fear of being embarrassed lasted up until the moment we located the swimming pool, and I saw the girl in the pink bikini. It was as if time stood still and everything around me moved in slow motion at the sight of this beautiful girl with long black hair, brown eyes, and skin like the foam on a mocha cappuccino. As I watched her play with a boy who was close to my age, I forgot to breathe. I didn't feel threatened by the boy, because it was clear to me that they were family. My cousin Stevie, who was cognizant of time and oblivious to the girl, continued to walk as I stood in place.

Stevie walked for approximately ten feet without noticing I was not by his side. As he reached the end of the walkway, he turned to talk to me and realized he left me near the entrance to the swimming pool. He stared at me with his eyebrows turned inward and a look of bewilderment.

"Vernon!" A moment passed, and I didn't respond.

"Monkey!" he yelled. I ignored him caught in a trance.

"Yellow Monkey!" I broke my stare and nodded at him. "Come on man, you know we have fifteen minutes. I'm not trying to hear my name, our description on the loud speaker, and get embarrassed out here." I put one finger in the air, tilted my head, and looked in the direction of the beautiful girl in the pink bikini. Stevie then realized why I stopped and stood frozen. He smiled and walked back to where I stood and joined me.

"Oh, she is bad, cousin," Stevie said as he spotted the girl of my admiration.

"Simply beautiful, man," I replied, and then shook hands with Stevie as a gesture of agreement. Stevie knew that before the week was over, I would try to get to know this girl, and he was willing to assist in the process.

This girl in the pink bikini, whose name I later learned was Jennifer, looked different from the girls who attended my school in Chicago. Jennifer was "an American who identified as White," and the first one I met who was my age. She wore a bikini swimsuit, which was forbidden in my home. Growing up in a strict Christian home my sisters were not allowed to wear bikini swimming suits; my mother believed they were nothing more than underwear and inappropriate for public spaces. As I made these observations and contemplated these ideas, Stevie and I forgot about our fifteen-minute time limit.

We soon heard three beeps over the loudspeaker, which signaled a pending public announcement. Next, we heard the voice of my Aunt Mignon. "This message is for Yellow, I mean, Vernon and Stevie who are approximately 5'1 and 5'3 in height. Vernon is wearing blue jeans and a Chicago Bulls' t-shirt. Stevie has on a pair of blue jeans and a t-shirt with an illustration of the Chicago skyline on the front. Security and others, if you see them walking near the pool, please escort them to the restaurant, because they are now late. Vernon and Stevie, if you can hear this, I love you." The announcement ended with the sound of my Aunt Mignon making a kissing sound over the loudspeaker. All of the children in the swimming pool erupted in laughter, as it was painfully evident that we were the intended targets of the message.

We ran back to the table to find my aunt and uncle laughing and enjoying a conversation. It was apparent by the looks on their faces they knew where we were and simply enjoyed embarrassing us in front of other children.

Uncle Bruce was the first to speak. "Didn't we tell you to get back here within fifteen minutes?"

In unison, Stevie and I responded, "Yes."

Aunt Mignon added, "Why weren't you here within fifteen minutes?"

"We were looking at some kids play near the pool," I said. "I'm sorry, and it will not happen again." I did not give any additional details about the cause of our late return to the table, but I continued to think about the girl who caught my attention.

Jennifer was beautiful, and I believed she was someone who I needed to get to know during that vacation. Yes, I was only in the fourth grade, but I had a superficial idea of the physical attributes I was attracted to in the opposite sex. Jennifer was a girl with long black hair, a slim physique, brown eyes, and a great smile. I simply thought Jennifer was pretty and I wanted to hold her hand, buy her a lollipop, kiss her on the cheek, or do whatever was appropriate for fourth grade. I had innocent intentions.

Relationships were not serious endeavors or long-term at this point in my life. I was hoping to make Jennifer my girlfriend for the week I was in Florida. With my cousin's assistance, I believed it was possible. We needed a strategic plan to get away from the adults and alone with Jennifer. After dinner that evening in the restaurant, I talked to Stevie about the plan that I envisioned would work to capture the affection and attention of Jennifer.

Video games were the solution. We believed if we could befriend the boy who was with Jennifer and invite him to the condo to play games, I would have the opportunity to learn about my crush. Stevie and I also believed that getting to know this other boy would enable me to acquire an ally in Jennifer. We thought about all possible scenarios, and this was the best option. The only challenge was to find the boy who was with my future wife for the week.

It was happenstance or perhaps destiny that the next day we went to the pool, Jennifer and her cousin were also there with family. I smiled at the sight of her and thought we could not have picked a better time to come to the pool. She was playing catch with a couple of other kids on the shallow end of the pool.

I looked at Stevie to begin the plan. "Do you see who I see?"

"Yes, the love of your life," Stevie said and followed-up with laughter.

I punched him in the shoulder. "Come on man. Get serious. It's time to put our earlier plan with video games into action."

"Ok, let's ask them if we can play."

Stevie and I waited for what seemed like a lifetime for the right time to ask for permission to join the game. The moment arrived when the ball accidentally flew in our direction. I picked up the ball and threw it back, but I was too afraid to ask if we could join their game. They said thanks and continued to play among themselves for another fifteen minutes when the ball traveled again in our direction. I may have missed the mark the first time, but I was not going to miss the opportunity for a second time. I picked up the ball and asked to play; a boy in the group responded "sure." I threw the ball back to their end of the pool and swam over with Stevie to introduce myself.

The boy said, "I'm John, and this is my cousin Jennifer."

I was in a frozen state with being this close to Jennifer and so for a moment I forgot how to speak. Thankfully, Stevie responded on our behalf. "I am Stevie, and this is my cousin Vernon." I missed my cue to say hello because I was focused on Jennifer with tunnel vision. It was as if everyone in the pool disappeared except for this beautiful girl wearing a pink bikini and me.

Stevie said "Yellow!"

I offered no response.

"Yellow, Yellow Monkey!" Stevie repeated.

I turned and looked at him with the look of disgust. He knew I hated that nickname and yet he used it in the presence of my crush.

John asked, "Yellow Monkey?" Then John and Jennifer laughed as if it were the funniest joke they had ever heard in their life. I was embarrassed and gave Stevie a look that communicated my anger and resentment. That moment at the pool was my first interaction with Jennifer, and I wanted to impress her.

As we played together, I discovered John and I had a lot in common. We were the same age and shared similar interests in video games, sports, and girls. He lived in Georgia and had four sisters. John was the only boy who traveled with his family, and so he was excited to spend time with other boys also. Over the course of a couple of days, we developed a good friendship that I hoped would extend beyond the week in Florida.

Near the end of our trip, while John, Stevie and I were playing video games, I decided it was time to let John in on my secret. I said, "I like your cousin. Do you think you could ask her how she feels about me?"

"I knew you liked her and I was just waiting for you to admit it."

"Is it that obvious?"

"Yes, every time that you are around her it's like you can't keep your eyes off her." Apparently, I was not good at hiding my feelings. John and I developed a good friendship in this short time, and so he agreed to put in a word to Jenifer.

I was confident that the response from Jennifer would be positive because I was popular among the girls in Chicago. My sisters may have teased me and called me Yellow Monkey, but I didn't experience many challenges when it came to attracting girls at my school, church, or in the neighborhood. I was confident that I could convince Jennifer to be my girlfriend for the remainder of my time in Florida. There would be an opportunity to hold her hand and possibly land a kiss. I thought it was just a matter of time, before Jennifer and I connected on a romantic level.

The following day after my confession to John, Stevie and I decided to go to the pool. I made plans to meet with John in an inadvertent attempt to also meet with Jennifer. She was often with him whenever he went to the pool. When we arrived at the pool, John was there, but Jennifer was not.

"Where is Jennifer?" I asked.

In a condescending voice, John said, "Don't worry, she will be here."

I followed up with my question and asked if he had an opportunity to talk with her. He said, "No, but I will when she gets here in a second."

My anticipation for her arrival was building as I attempted to distract myself with swim races between Stevie, John, and me. I didn't know how to swim, so I went up and down the shallow end of the pool with a combination of doggy paddling and running. The thirty minutes I waited for Jennifer felt like hours. Eventually, she walked into the indoor pool facilities and time once again stood still.

Jennifer came to the poolside, immediately smiled at John, and said hello. She also acknowledged me and Stevie with a slight grin. I briefly replied with a smile and then went underwater not to show how happy I was to see her. I figured this was the best strategy to play it cool and keep her guessing about my intentions. As she walked away from the pool to talk to her mom, John, Stevie, and I returned to race on the shallow end. At one point, I managed to make it to an end of the pool with John, and that's when I asked him to go and talk to her for me. He agreed.

Stevie and I continued to play as we waited for John to return. My aunt and uncle sat in the pool lounge chairs to keep a close eye on us. About ten minutes later John came back to the pool. As John walked up, I could read his body language which indicated that something was wrong. He had his head down and would not make eye contact with me.

"John, what's up?" I asked. I could tell Jennifer's response was not positive before he opened his mouth to speak. I braced myself for the rejection.

John didn't look at me. He said, "Well I talked to my cousin, and she thinks you're a nice guy and all, but you're colored." As the word "colored" came out of his mouth, he turned and ran away.

I'm not sure if he thought I was going to punch him, but I stood there and whispered to myself, "colored?" An inner dialogue continued as I thought about the significance of the word "colored?" Wasn't that something that my parents and grandparents were called? Who calls people colored? This is the 90s. What do you mean "colored?" In my head, I searched for meaning in Jennifer's choice of words. I thought labeling people as colored, was something from the 1950s and 60s. My parents grew up during the era of the United States when it was common practice to have separate water fountains, public restrooms, schools, and other public accommodations. Racism was overt in the "separate but equal" world of my parents. I didn't believe race still mattered in the same way it did for my parents.

Before this experience, I realized that I was a Black boy. I simply did not give it much thought because everyone in my environment was Black. As a young person growing up in segregated Chicago, I didn't see how the color of my skin was significant in my relationships with other children. Sure, I was teased and called Yellow by my friends and sisters. However, this was the first time my color, race, was used by a White peer to justify different treatment towards me. Jennifer's response was my first interaction with the understanding how some Whites perceived me due to my identity as a Black boy.

Before this spring break during the fourth grade, I didn't understand how race influenced friendships or romantic interests. I saw a beautiful girl, and while I acknowledged she looked physically different than the girls from my neighborhood, I didn't care. In fact, because she was different from what I was used to, it made her that much more attractive. Instead of teaching me to swim, Jeniffer pushed me toward drowning in the inferiority messages of Black male identity in America.

We are valued when we have a ball or microphone in our hand, but otherwise, in many instances, we are perceived as inferior. Black males are praised for their expertise in professional athletics, music, and other forms of entertainment. However, outside of those realms, Black males are associated with criminal behavior, academic underachievement, and in this case during my fourth-grade year of school, an undesirable love interest. While I had significant pride in myself and my community, this incident exposed me to the reality that to be Black in America is often a marker of inferiority.

Jennifer did not want to reciprocate any feelings of attraction toward me because somewhere in her experiences she was told that Black boys were not suitable romantic partners. Her education, informed by racism, convinced her that Blackness was synonymous with people less than her race. It was impossible for her to see beyond the color of my skin. In the immediacy and anger after Jennifer's rejection, I thought all White people did not like and respect Black America.

The next morning I was still really upset with Jennifer. Evidence of my anger revealed itself when I gave the middle finger to a White couple when they drove down the street and decided to stare at my cousin and me while we stood outside to wait for my aunt and uncle. Due to my experiences the previous day, I believed this couple looked at us as if they had never seen Black people. I was trying to make sense of Jennifer's response and told myself that maybe she had never met a Black person before that trip.

I thought the White couples' stare was suggestive of a belief that Black families did not belong in that community. My experiences at the pool the day before caused me to react with this mindset. Angry, upset, and feeling less-valued, I believed that my middle finger was the best way to say good morning to this couple that stared in my direction. I gave them my middle finger at the exact moment my aunt walked out of the house. She caught me with my middle finger raised high in the air, standing firm and making direct eye contact with the White man who was a passenger in the golf cart.

"Vernon! What are you doing?" I tried to play if off like I was stretching. My Aunt Mignon was not a fool and my cousin Stevie could not stop laughing.

I stuttered as I attempted to push the words from my brain to my lips. It was useless, because there was no way I could've talked myself out what she witnessed. I was in trouble, and so I put my head down, accepted my fate, and climbed into the backseat of the car.

My uncle came rushing out of the house after hearing my aunt yell my name. He thought something had happened to me and didn't understand why she screamed. They talked for a while quietly outside of the car before my uncle entered the driver's seat. As we pulled away from the house, they swapped turns lecturing me about my decision that morning.

For the full hour it took for us to drive from the timeshare to the theme park, I was unable to say a word in my defense. I didn't think there was anything that I could say to excuse my decision to give the finger to the White couple. The previous twenty-four hours planted the seeds of racial inferiority within me and were beginning to harvest in my refusal to use my voice. An individual act of racism silenced my mind and my ability to speak.

My aunt and uncle were not aware of what I was experiencing at that moment. I was breathing Black rage in and out of my lungs when I exhaled my middle finger toward that White man in the golf cart. It was the moment when I realized the social implications beyond my community that came with the racial classification of Black in the United States. Because I lived in a racially segregated community and attended a predominately Black school, Blackness was my norm, and I didn't give it much thought.

I was teased for my color, and I participated in name calling toward my sisters based on differences in skin color. Yellow Monkey was the name my sisters gave me and others used, due to physical features. I joined others and called my sister Melanie, Blackie. Nonetheless, I didn't quite understand colorism or the negative implications associated with my race. The rejection I received from Jennifer alongside the stare received from the White couple on the following day, was the start of a shift in the perspective of me and my community.

I was unable to articulate my discovery in self-awareness during the fourth grade trip to Florida, but something inside me changed. When we reached the theme park, I was punished. I had to sit by the pool and write "I will not give adults the middle finger" fifty times. While I wrote, my cousin had the time of his life riding the roller coasters, eating junk food, and playing games. I watched with envy and thought about Jennifer who was beautiful yet simultaneously ugly because she believed I was inferior due to the color of my skin. That spring break experience taught me that racism was alive, well, and strong enough to run an infinite number of marathons in a row.

How does this story reveal pathways to systemic problems and the experiences of Black males?

During spring break of my fourth-grade year in school, I became aware of how some "Americans who identify as White" internalized racism and projected their misguided beliefs toward others. I felt sad, angry, and embarrassed, when Jennifer decided that she was not interested in being my girlfriend for the week! Yes, it was a minor fourth-grade romance, but it did reveal the perceptions of me held by some of my White peers. My experiences with racist beliefs in the fourth grade are symptomatic of the more significant structural implications of ideas, laws, and policies that continue to support notions of inherent racial inferiority and the criminalization of Black males.

The Michael Brown case is one recent incident that confirms how premature beliefs about Black males influence justice in the legal system. Officer Darren Wilson claimed he decided to kill rather than to arrest unarmed Michael Brown because he feared for his life. This fear was based on Brown's size and race. Brown may have made some poor decisions before his interaction with Wilson, but they did not justify the homicide where his body laid on the street for four and a half hours in Fergusson, Missouri (Lowery, 2016). However, Wilson's claim of fear alongside inconsistent testimonies and a historically racially biased court system cleared him of any violation of rights (Eckholm & Apuzzo, 2015). The court confirmed once again that the lives of Black males possess little to no value in the United States.

Another homicide that preceded Michael Brown's case involved a young Black male, Trayvon Martin, and George Zimmerman, a former civilian neighborhood security officer. Zimmerman initiated contact with Martin, because he was a Black male who wore a hoodie sweatshirt and fit a preconceived belief that he was a criminal suspect. Similar to Wilson, Zimmerman claimed that fear was the rationale for a response with deadly force. This notion of self-defense coupled with Florida's *Stand Your Ground* law enabled Zimmerman to murder Martin without penalty (Coates, 2013). In the Brown and Martin cases, the common thread is that the perpetrators possessed beliefs consistent with racism that devalued the lives of Black males.

A police officer or civilian who was indoctrinated in an education system and raised in an environment like Jennifer is taught from a young age that Black males are worthless. These ideas of inherent racial inferiority are planted as children and bloom among adults. They influence how officers and patrolmen secure the streets. The devaluation of Black males' lives and their association with criminal behavior support racial profiling and in some instances homicides that are not penalized.

When schools use an irrelevant curriculum, support educational models that emphasize standardized tests, and do not provide Black males with opportunities for their voices to be heard we strengthen and maintain racism. It is crucial that we build positive self-awareness among young Black boys to empower them to serve as agents of change. Systems of racism are created by individuals like Jennifer who possess beliefs that race can serve as an adequate measure to determine a person's value.

Harris (1995) states that in US society, Whiteness acts as a property right and people who are identified as White are often granted reputation rights that people of color cannot access. As a young Black male, I was unable to gain association with the positive reputation that accompanies someone who fits the definition of Whiteness in the United States. In Jennifer's words, I was "colored" and therefore not suitable for a puppy love romance with a White girl.

Jennifer's comments about me reveal how children can adopt such belief systems that if unchallenged can lead to the reproduction of inequalities based on race. When I entered the fifth grade, my family moved from Chicago to a south suburban community called South Holland. At my new school, I learned more about the assumptions that some of my White peers had about me due to my perceived biological differences. I desperately wanted to be myself, and simultaneously I wanted to be liked by everyone. This desire to be popular and attract the attention of girls like Jennifer led to school suspensions and other conflicts with school authority.

To download the FREE PDF workbook and instructional guide, please visit: www.vlindsayphd.com/crtblackmales

References

Coates, T. (2013). How stand your ground relates to George Zimmerman. *The Atlantic*. Published July 16, 2013 and Retrieved November 20, 2017 from https://www.theatlantic.com/national/archive/2013/07/how-stand-your-ground-relates-to-george-zimmerman/277829/

Coates, T. (2015). *Between the world and me*. New York, NY: Spiegel and Grau.

Delgado, R. (2000). Storytelling for oppositionists and others: A plea for narrative. In R. Delgado & J. Stefancic (Eds.), *Critical race theory: The cutting edge*. Philadelphia, PA: Temple University Press.

Eckholm, E., & Apuzzo, M. (2015). Darrien Wilson is cleared of rights violations in Fergusson Shooting. *The New York Times*. Published March 4, 2015 and Retrieved November 20, 2017 from https://www.nytimes.com/2015/03/05/us/darren-wilson-is-cleared-of-rights-violations-in-ferguson-shooting.html

Harris, C. I. (1995). Whiteness as property. In K. Crenshaw, N. Gotanda, & K. Thomas (Eds.), *Critical race theory: The key writings that formed the movement* (pp. 276–291). New York, NY: New Press.

Holzman, M. (2012). National Summary. In J. Jackson, A. Beaudry, E. Dexter, & T. K.Watson (Eds.), *The urgency of now: The Schott 50 state report on public education and Black males 2012* (pp. 1–56). Cambridge, MA: Schott Foundation of Public Education. Retrieved November 16, 2017 from http://blackboysreport.org/bbreport2012.pdf

Lowery, W. (2016). *They can't kill us all: Ferguson, Baltimore, and a new era in America's racial justice movement*. New York, NY: Little, Brown, and Company.

Swaine, J., Laughland, O., Lartey, J., & McCarthy, C. (2015). *Young Black men killed by US police at highest rate in year of 1,134 deaths*. Retrieved November 16, 2017 from https://www.theguardian.com/us-news/2015/dec/31/the-counted-police-killings-2015-young-black-men

Yosso, J. T. (2006). *Critical race counterstories along the Chicano/Chicano educational pipeline*. New York, NY: Routledge Taylor and Francis Group.

· 3 ·

THE THUG AND ME

Introduction

I hated being called a pretty boy as a child. Girls were pretty, and I was "all boy." I climbed trees, had fist fights, caught frogs, played in the dirt with bugs, ate beef, and participated in sports. As far as I was concerned, there was nothing pretty about me! However, people used to say that because my eyelashes were so long, I looked like a girl who wore mascara. I believed such comments coupled with my family's move to South Holland insulted the image I wanted to project as a young Black boy.

Throughout much of my adolescence, I admired other Black boys who dressed and behaved in alignment with the counterculture to conservatism. They sagged their pants, used profane language, sought validation through violence, listened to and modeled their lives after mainstream hip-hop music, often categorized as gangster rap, and lived in cities. I desperately wanted to be a thug, because they were often correlated with words such as dangerous, tough, popular, and fearless. My father, a Christian minister, stressed the importance of participating in church and put less emphasis on the approval of my peers.

In many ways, I did not fit the definition of a thug, but I tried. I sagged my pants, fought other boys, listened to gangster rap, and did whatever I could to attract the respect I believed followed others who did not conform to their parents' expectations. I misperceived gangsta status, recognition as courageous and tough, as central to my identity.

Due to the flood of images presented in television, film, music and my environment I thought there were tangible benefits for Black boys who others regarded as thugs. My parents wanted something else for my life, but I remained attracted to the lure of poisonous popular images and association with peers who subscribed to the dominant depictions of Black male identity. Thugs had power, money, the respect among other boys, and an abundance of girlfriends.

I believed my family's move from Chicago to South Holland would ruin my lofty dreams of the "thug life" that was central to the music of Tupac Shakur. The move to the suburbs was one more strike against the chances for me to achieve association with what I believed was an authentic identity for Black boys. My father was always active in my life, a pillar of the community, and the furthest thing from a thug. Well maybe he was a thug for Jesus, but I sought validation among my friends. I wanted to reflect what I listened to in music and saw via television and film. Life in the suburbs did not support the identity that I believed was normative for Black boys my age.

In the narrative that follows, my goal is not to vilify Hip-Hop or rap music. The claim that Hip-Hop makes a negative impact on the lives of Black males is too often repeated by conservatives and refuted by research (Coates, 2017; Dyson, 2005; Jeffries & Jeffries, 2017; Travis, 2013). I aim to demonstrate how the music of Tupac, my friends, environment and my father influenced my performance of masculinity in the transition from life on the Southside of Chicago to the south suburbs.

The Thug and Me

So much of my identity was tied to Chatham, my neighborhood friends, and the local school I attended, that I had mixed emotions about moving from the city to the suburbs with my family. While I was excited about experiencing a new neighborhood, I was afraid of being taken away from the life I knew in the city. The decision to move was guided by my parents' dreams, fears, and desires.

My parents were fearful of the crimes that threatened the lives of Black boys in Chicago and believed relocating to the suburbs would remove negative influences. I remember being told that a part of the decision to move was a growing concern that I would have the desire to join a gang. Their concerns were not irrational, because one of my sisters began in junior high school to demonstrate signs of getting involved in gang related activity. She was hanging with the wrong crowd and engaging self-destructive activities such as stealing from stores and skipping school. My parents were concerned that I would also get negatively influenced by my peers and follow a similar path.

It was already becoming cool among my friends to know the handshakes and the different abbreviations for local gangs. GD stood for Gangster Disciples and they primarily wore clothes with black and blue colors. I was sometimes teased and praised, because my initials, VL, were also the abbreviation for GD's rival gang called the Vice Lords. During the years my family lived in Chicago I was never approached to join either gang, but I had friends with older brothers who claimed gang affiliation.

It was common to hear my friends glorify crimes and to discuss the importance of joining a gang. One of the arguments was that gangs offered protection and an extended family. To my ears at this time, it sounded like a rational way of thinking about the benefits of joining one of the infamous street organizations. The reality was I had plenty of family and I lived in a moderately safe community; joining a gang was not going to offer me anything I didn't already possess. My parents decided to relocate to keep me and my sisters from getting caught up in activities that inevitably could result in prison or premature death.

Before moving to South Holland, I believed that all White people were part of a close and connected community. My fifth-grade mentality had me convinced that because they shared the same skin color, everyone knew each other and they were friends or family. That wasn't the case in my community, and I didn't make the connection to people who are identified as White.

Life in the suburbs revealed some persistent fears in my life. I was concerned about losing my friends and the challenges I would face in a new environment. Fighting was among the tools I used to validate myself, and I thought about the inevitability of meeting someone stronger and faster than me. I was fearful of the necessity to demonstrate the behaviors I claimed were critical to my life.

I believed Black boys, including myself, should claim membership in illegal street organizations, sell drugs, and pursue multiple girlfriends. Although my experiences and friends told a different story of life as a Black boy, I was convinced self-defeating behaviors were central to my identity. One of the major influences in my life was commercialized rap music that glorified illegal activity, the drug culture, and women as sexual objects. I approached my new life in the suburbs down a road in search of peers who would validate me as a thug.

The move ignited a fire in my performance of the thug role that I perceived as assigned to me as a Black boy born in the United States. I felt a desperate desire to prove my self-worth at school, at home, and in my suburban community. Between the ages of 10–18, I was suspended twice from school, had numerous arguments with my parents, experimented with cigarettes and alcohol, stole *Playboy* magazines from the gas station, and enjoyed fist fights. One of the major influences in my life was mainstream rap music that is often incorrectly labeled as Hip-Hop.

Hip-Hop is a culture that spawned from the struggles of Black and Latino/a youth in New York's South Bronx. With the construction of the Cross-Bronx Expressway and fires that destroyed a significant number of homes in communities occupied by Black and Puerto Rican residents, Hip-Hop began as a tool to create awareness and build resistance (Chang, 2007). At block parties where emcees, DJs, graffiti artists, and B-boys/girls convened, Hip-Hop enabled community and positive self-expression. Rap is an element of Hip-Hop that has been adopted by dominant media outlets to support consumerism and behaviors that often debase and less frequently uplift communities of color.

In my adolescence, I didn't understand the dichotomy between Hip-Hop and rap music; I was a young Black male with great respect and admiration for Tupac Shakur. Tupac's music had a significant impression on how I believed that I needed to behave. I equated being tough and the willingness to fight anyone who challenged me as critical personality traits. The political and socially conscious themes in some of Tupac's music were disregarded. Instead, I identified with the tracks that reflected misogyny and crime such as *Hail Mary*, *Nothing but a Gangsta Party* and *I Get Around.*

The music and my friends enabled me to serve as a teacher and student of popular notions of masculinity. I taught my friends effective strategies to sweep, kick, and punch opponents during the moments we managed to escape our parents' supervision. They taught me that losing is not an option when it came to sports. I taught them that being called a girl was the most horrific insult on the planet! They taught me that identifying as a thug was masculine and it fit our identities as Black boys.

My friends and I swapped ideas and behaviors that reflected dominant negative depictions of race, racism, and masculinity. As Black boys, we were socialized into believing that because of our race we were destined to lives full of crime. Our sources for inspiration were older boys on the playground, movies, and music. I was one of the young brothers that Hutchinson (1996) claimed was convinced by films such as *Boyz N The Hood* that being a Black male was synonymous with gangster life. Anything that we consumed was fair game for application in our lives as Black boys with the desire to meet masculinity standards, and those beliefs stayed with me in the move to South Holland.

On moving day, I was allowed to spend time with three of my friends who lived within a two block radius of my home. Matthew, Mark, and Herman were some of my closest friends growing up, and we enjoyed the music of Tupac and sports. We spent a considerable amount of time trying to mimic Tupac and other rappers' style, playing basketball, baseball, and our unique boy version of tag. Of all the things, we attempted to cram in on the day my family moved to South Holland; I remember our final game of tag.

This was not an ordinary game of hide and seek, where one person counts and everyone else finds a simple place to hide like a closet or underneath a table. As boys we needed to amplify it to another level, so we looked for the most dangerous places in the neighborhood to hide. Our version of tag could not be contained indoors; it included the alleys, backyards, and garages of our neighborhood.

My favorite place to hide was on the roof of my friend Mark's garage. It was located in the backyard of his house, and the main service door faced the alley. It was adjacent to a tree with low branches that served as a ladder for us to climb to the roof. Whenever we played tag, I would often climb the tree and hide on the side of the roof that was concealed from the backyard.

On this particular day, our game went in a different direction of exploring the fearlessness that I embraced as a Black boy in search of validation as a thug. At one point of the game, my friend Herman was "it," and I was camped out in my favorite hiding place. When Herman found me, I was stuck in a position with no feasible way to get down without being tagged. The only option was to jump off the roof and hopefully land on the other side of Mark's neighbor's six-foot fence. Without hesitation, I jumped.

When I hit the ground on the other side of the fence, I did an army roll like I had seen so many times in the films. My friends laughed and said "dang Vernon! You ain't' no joke." I said yup as I stood up and felt the pain in my right arm and legs. My arm was bleeding, and I couldn't quite put my weight entirely on my legs. I wanted to cry, but as a boy, I knew the penalty of showing emotions in a public space.

Instead of crying, I asked for a timeout and went inside Mark's house to clean up my arm. Away from my boys, I cried, because I was in a lot of pain and probably should have gone to see a doctor. After five minutes, I quickly wiped away my tears, stopped the bleeding on my arm, and went back outside, to find my friends who were on top of the garage's roof I barely escaped. By the looks on their faces, I could tell they were building the energy and courage to jump from the garage. I should have immediately returned inside to get Mark's parents, but my friends would have called me a punk or worse, a girl. The best option for me was to join my three friends for another jump.

I climbed the tree to the roof. On our last day together, we bonded through the injuries we sustained jumping from Mark's garage. Thankfully, our scrapes, burns, and pulled muscles were not serious. Each of us fought our tears in fear of violating the code of masculinity that forbids boys from showing emotions and anything that might make us look vulnerable. We were a tight-knit group bonded by social constructs we did not know existed. Later that afternoon, I thought about the likelihood of finding a similar circle of friends in my new neighborhood. Matthew, Mark, and Herman were the types of friends that I would do anything for just like Tupac described in his song, *If My Homie Call*.

At the end of our last day together, Herman's mom drove my friends and me to my new home in suburbia. In the car, I had to suppress another set of mixed emotions. I was happy to be at the start of a new adventure, but I was sad to leave my friends and the familiarity of my old neighborhood. In the backseat of my friend's car, I looked out of the window, fought my tears, and talked about how different the suburbs appeared from the city. When we made it to South Holland, I talked about the smooth sidewalks and likened them to a paradise for bikes, rollerblades, and skateboards.

I also thought about what it would be like to have friends and neighbors who were White. Growing up in a racially segregated Chicago community did not offer much opportunity for interactions with people outside of my racial group. Due to my experiences in Florida with Jennifer, I believed it would be difficult to make genuine friends who were White. I did not think that all White people were evil or despised Black people, but I was convinced that there would be some people who would not like me based merely on my race.

After driving for thirty minutes, we pulled up to the house, and everyone in the car was impressed. One of my friends asked, "Monkey, what did y'all win the lottery or something?" Occasionally my friends would also call me Yellow Monkey or Monkey for short because they knew my sisters used this name for me and they thought it was funny. The size of the home we were moving into was significantly larger than my previous house. I knew that my parents had to borrow money to help the church buy the home, but I didn't know the details, so I just laughed. We climbed out of the car, denying our pain from our earlier jumps and walked to the front door of my new home.

From the outside the house looked like a miniature replica of The White House in Washington, DC; it had two long white pillars that gave it incredible curb appeal. When my friends and I entered the home, we immediately saw a massive glass chandelier that hung from the ceiling in the foyer. It looked expensive and made an impression that this was a wealthy family's home. The house had a joint living and dining room separated by four six-foot white pillars that resembled the set on the outside of the home.

My home in South Holland had everything my family needed and desired. It had a spacious eat-in kitchen, five bedrooms, separate laundry quarters, three full bathrooms and a finished basement. The house also had an attached garage that looked comparable in size to the one in Mark's family's backyard. I knew it wouldn't be long before I tested the pull of gravity from atop my new garage. I just needed to make some friends.

We moved into the home in July and school began in August. The time allowed me a month to prepare for the transition to a new school. I was excited and anxious as my first day at McKinley Junior High School approached. At my former school, I was popular and had plenty of friends. I was hoping that I could duplicate a similar experience in the fifth grade.

When I started school in the suburbs, still operating under the dichotomy of my father's and my friends' understandings of masculinity, I worked hard to express the boy who I had come to know. My father taught me that practicing discipline, demonstrating respect for adults, and working hard in school were the values I should possess. However, I was more drawn to the ideas that excelling in sports, undermining school, and fighting were the keys to open doors that allowed me to fully express myself. I believed school was primarily for socializing with my peers; learning and respecting my teachers occupied secondary and tertiary positions among goals.

To my surprise, my suburban school nearly had the same amount of students of color as White students. Nonetheless, I had a difficult time trying to fit in and initially find friends. My new classmates did not know of my alternative name, Yellow Monkey, and I was grateful. However, my new peers did find ways to challenge me as the new kid who thought he was a thug.

On a day I left my baseball hat on the lunch table, another boy picked it up and decided to test me. My baseball hat that I never wore with the brim forward complemented the pants I often wore sagged; they served as props for the thug role I performed when with my friends. I wasn't a part of any gang, but I believed wearing my hat to the right, left, or backward conveyed the message that I was tough and able to defend myself.

Well, apparently in the fifth grade, wearing a baseball hat in any direction other than forward also relayed I was just a fake wannabe thug. On one day I was playing with a group of friends during recess when I heard someone call my name from the other side of the playground. "Hey yo, Vernon! I have your hat." He stood there in the middle of the field dangling my hat by his pinkie finger and a sinister grin on his face. I left my hat on the lunch table, and he picked it up with the intention to tease me and test the thug reputation I was desperately trying to make in my new school. As I walked over to grab my hat, he dropped it on the ground, stepped on it, and looked directly into my eyes, for emphasis.

At that moment, I remembered something I heard in Tupac's song *Tha Lunatic*, and a series of thoughts and actions followed. I thought this guy was trying to play me like the Nintendo video game mentioned in *Tha Lunatic*, meaning he didn't respect me and he wanted to see how I would respond. My evidence lay in his decision to step on my hat in the middle of the playground. I couldn't ignore it, let it slide, and look for the nearest adult for help.

For a moment, I transported myself into a different world when I saw my hat being stepped on from the other side of the playground. Everything around me slowed down, and I focused my eyes and attention on the head of the boy who just called me out in front of my new peers who I wanted to impress. I ran directly toward him, jumped into the air because like most of my peers he was taller than me, and I punched him right in the face. It was like a scene from a movie because after feeling the impact of my punch, he fell to the ground.

This brief fight was a defining moment for me in the fifth grade and my new life in South Holland. Everyone laughed at the boy who stumbled to the ground, and I gained a reputation for being tough (along with a trip to the principal's office). The principal gave me the spin about the importance of keeping my hands to myself and making positive, non-violent choices to resolve a conflict. He also called home and told my parents of the incident.

My sisters laughed and teased me for getting in trouble again at my new school. I didn't have a good response to this one, and so instead I just looked in their direction and told them to "shut-up." I had not finished a full month in my new school, and somehow I managed to find trouble. Unfortunately, that was not the only time a classmate attempted to see if I was as tough as I portrayed myself.

The day after the fight, I was in lunch, and another boy tried to test me. He took my lunch and then laughed it off with another student who was sitting next to him. It was as if he didn't hear about my altercation on the playground the previous day. Maybe he did and just decided it was his turn to teach me a lesson. From the seeds of masculinity planted in me by my father, friends, and schooling experiences when I lived in Chatham, I knew that I could not afford to ignore this boy's decision to take my food.

My immediate response was not violence. I was already on a punishment at home for the fight over my hat the previous day. So, I decided to give him a loud and clear verbal warning. I said, "Give me my lunch. I'm not a punk and I will knock you out!" I was not really tough, but I knew how to play the part.

The kid who stole my lunch laughed at my threat and continued to talk with the person sitting next to him. At that moment, it was clear to me that I needed to provide a demonstration. I put my embarrassment, anger, and frustration into my fists and turned toward violence.

I channeled the energy of the former heavyweight boxing champion of the world, Mike Tyson, and my favorite rapper, Tupac. I threw what felt like a thousand punches in under one minute. My fists were rapidly swinging as Pac claimed in his song *Violent*, where he rhymes about physical retaliation toward a racist cop. I tried to use 1/8 of the power that Tyson possessed in his infamous fights that didn't make it beyond the first round. Although, I wasn't strong like Tupac or Tyson the boy quickly returned my lunch. Everyone at the lunch table sang in unison, "Dang."

My mission was accomplished among my peers, and I furthered my reputation as one who wouldn't back down. After this sixty seconds display of how fast I could punch, one student said: "Vernon got them hands." It was his way of complimenting me and letting others know that I knew how to fight. Tears started to form in the boy's eyes who took my lunch. He passed it back to me and said, "I was only playing man." I felt sympathy for approximately a millisecond. Fighting was how I convinced myself I would attract the right type of friends in my first year of school in the suburbs.

In the sixth grade, I continued my activities from the fifth grade and began to associate with some boys who were on a similar path to me with regards to getting in trouble at school and going against our parents' desires. This group of guys smoked cigarettes and frequently stole small items from local gas stations and stores. Many of my peers recognized them as the "cool guys," but only a selected few would dare to be seen with them away from school. I was among the few students who would hang with them during and after school.

The leader of the group was a White boy named Dan. He wasn't a part of any gang, but like my classmates from the city his brothers claimed affiliation. Dan and I first bonded through basketball. He could match my jump shot and keep up with me on the court. We also connected through a similar interest in girls and music. With Dan and the guys, I learned of boundaries in the suburbs and how to present an inauthentic version of myself.

Near my home, there was a community called Thornton that developed a reputation for residents who supported white supremacy. There were rumors of racists police officers, skinheads and other members of neo-Nazi groups that lived in this town. Happenstance or not, Thornton was one of Dan's favorite places to visit after school. We were in the sixth grade, but Dan managed to attract a girlfriend who was in the seventh grade and lived in Thornton.

One day I decided to go with Dan to see his girlfriend after school. We rode our bikes through a set of popular forest trails near my home and along the way we came across a path that led underneath an expressway viaduct. On the concrete walls of the ramp, I saw Nazi Swastika symbols. The symbols were the first sign that I was entering a potentially volatile environment, but I continued without fear. Ignoring that Dan's identity afforded him privileges in this environment, I thought that if he felt comfortable going, there was no need for me to be afraid.

When we made it to Thornton and ultimately to Dan's girlfriend's house, I knew something was off within moments of ringing her doorbell. She said hello and then immediately whispered something that I couldn't hear in Dan's ear. We stayed at her house for about forty-five minutes, before Dan said it's time to go back to South Holland. On the ride back through the forest, he told me that it wasn't safe for me in Thornton after dark.

Dan's girlfriend's whispers to him were a warning that it was not a good idea to bring me into her community. She told him she wasn't supposed to have boys at her house while her parents were at work and the punishment would be more severe if her dad found a Black boy on her property. Dan tried to convince her I was ok, but she insisted we leave before sunset.

It was Dan's girlfriend's response that convinced me of Thornton's racist reputation. Her family was one among many residents who did not welcome Black people into their community. Like Jennifer who I met in the fourth grade on the spring break trip to Florida, this experience taught me that she was not the only White girl who prejudged my value due to race. It didn't matter how cool I thought I behaved, my identity as a Black boy was reason enough for hate.

After the experience in Thornton, I continued to hang out with Dan. I never felt that he held racist views towards me, but I felt awkward when he told me about the fun he experienced while in Thornton. The fun he enjoyed often excluded me, because it wasn't safe. Sure, I was invited and went with Dan on some occasions, but I didn't feel welcomed by his friends. I tried hard to fit in, but my Black skin often interfered with genuine acceptance.

The weight of peer pressure was too heavy for me to develop enough positive self-awareness that didn't require validation from my peers. The mentioned above forest trails that led to Thornton were among my favorite places in South Holland. It had multiple bike trails with hills that were extremely fun to ride. In these trails, I tried desperately to impress my new friends.

One day, with Dan and the guys who were notorious at my new school, we decided to ride our bikes through the forest trails. We were not going to Thornton, but to explore some hills that appeared dangerous. About midway through the forest, Dan stopped the crew. He offered each of us a cigarette. As someone who was diagnosed with asthma from an early age, I was aware of the associated health risks, my parents and teachers' warnings about cigarettes, but I was desperate for Dan's approval. Each of my friends accepted the cigarettes without hesitation, so I also followed suit in fear of being labeled lame.

When Dan and I became friends, my family and I lived in South Holland for one year. I enjoyed spending time with Dan, but he couldn't replace my friends from my old neighborhood. We never played an extreme version of tag that involved jumping from our home garages, but we did other less intelligent activities to prove our compliance with the accepted norms of masculine behavior.

With Dan, I played with lighters and was suspended from school to prove I could hang with the guys. In the sixth grade, we found a lighter in the playground during recess. On a dare from one of my friends, I took the lighter and lit a piece of grass on fire. I got scared and immediately stepped out the flame, but it was too late because a teacher saw the smoke. Later that afternoon, I was suspended from school for playing with a lighter and nearly setting the field on fire. Thankfully, no one was injured or went to jail in my performances of masculinity with Dan, but I remained drawn to an image I believed others expected of me as a Black male who was born in Chicago.

The move to South Holland seemed to further my desire for a connection with hyper-masculine representations of Black males via the music of Tupac Shakur. Listening to his music was as much part of my daily routine as brushing my teeth. Tupac influenced me so much that sometimes I modeled by behaviors after him. He had "thug life" tattooed across his stomach, which motivated me to create pseudo business cards when I was in the sixth grade with my official title listed as thug. I folded bandannas and tied them across my forehead to mirror Tupac's images in his music videos and album covers. Tupac's music was a window to a world I desperately wanted to open and climb in for myself.

Although, Tupac had some songs that were positive and uplifting I was more interested in the tracks and other rappers who glorified crime and reinforced negative depictions of Black masculinity. Emcees who addressed current events, Black pride, Black history and culture to raise social awareness were corny. I enjoyed music that depicted Black males as murderers, drug dealers, and womanizers. My father exemplified and taught me a different version of manhood, but during my younger years I saw him as being old, out of touch with reality, and primarily focused on the needs of his church.

I spent nearly every Wednesday and Sunday in the church as a young person, but I refused to embrace my father's form of masculinity. At church, I learned that Jesus was "the truth, the way, and the light," and outside of the church, I found refuge in the lyrics of Tupac Shakur. Tupac was "the truth," and not because of tracks like Dear Momma, Keep Ya Head Up, or other classics, where he offered hope and an opportunity to make people aware of critical conditions facing the Black community. I admired Tupac because in many ways his music rejected everything that my parents and the church tried to instill in me.

My parents were not happy with my decision to listen to rap music, especially my father. One day in the sixth grade I remember coming home after school with headphones in my ear and listening to a Tupac album. My father and I got into a discussion about the music I was listening to that ended with him asking for every rap album I owned. I refused and he threatened me while chasing me around the basement of our home. My mother came to my rescue and convinced him to revisit the discussion at a later time when his temper was in a better place.

That evening, I went to sleep and had a vivid nightmare that involved the music I owned and my father. I dreamed I came home from school listening to Tupac as I always did when I found my father sitting at the table reading his Bible. We began to discuss the music I enjoyed, and an argument ensued similarly to what occurred earlier in the real world. The dream became a nightmare when he refused to accept that I would not hand him my music. He snapped, pulled a gun from his Bible, and instead of chasing me around the basement like he did in reality, he killed me.

When I woke up the next morning, my body was soaked in sweat, because of this nightmare where my father murdered me for listening to rap music. I showered, got dressed, and went to grab the compact disc (CD) player that I carried with me on my walk to school. I pressed play and received an error on the display screen. There was no disk in the player, and I was certain I left it there before bed. After searching for my music, I discovered my father took every rap album I owned and threw them away at an undisclosed location. I asked my father why he threw my CDs away and he replied, "I'm raising a man, not some thug."

When my family moved from Chicago to South Holland, my father took nearly every book that he kept in his home office. I believe that not only were the books symbolic of my dad's obsession with learning, but he used them as tools to counter my collection of rap CDs. In my father's books you found resources that informed his community work and influenced his positive relationship with my mom. My music validated participation in criminal activity and the accumulation of sexual partners. Due to my status as my parents' only boy, we moved to the suburbs in part to help me grow into manhood.

During the transition from the city to the burbs, I wanted validation from my peers and my father. My friends valued courage that manifested in activities such as jumping from home garages, fighting other boys, and getting in trouble at school. I did all of the above in the fifth and sixth grade. My dad valued strength and discipline which he exemplified at home and in his work at the church. He made it very clear that he did not want me to define myself through the lenses of Hip-Hop artists.

My father did instill in me that men take care of their responsibilities, work hard, provide for their families, create strong spiritual lives, and don't complain without also seeking solutions to their problems. He was not a perfect dad, and he did allow the construction of masculinity to influence how he interacted with me and my sisters. For example, he was not an affectionate father; he infrequently, if ever, said, "I Love you." He attempted to show his love through financially providing for my family, and moving to the suburbs, but he rarely verbalized his love. My dad was a good father; he was not aware of me and my siblings' social emotional needs.

In contrast to what I embraced in my family's transition from the city to the suburbs, my father taught me that I did not need to physically fight everyone to validate my self-worth. My father did his best to raise me in the church and to define my identity through a relationship with God. He didn't understand my obsession with Tupac and the need to prove myself as tough outside the congregation.

In moving to the suburbs, I sought acceptance through my physical strength and ability to fight other boys. I believed Tupac's public persona was the epitome of Black male identity and a model for my life. I believed my suburban school was not a place to learn, but a stage to perform a version of self-defeating Black masculinity that was not transformational.

What are the implications of this story and how can we redefine masculinity to encourage academic success for Black boys?

I never recovered the music my father took from me, but all these years later I understand he subscribed to a Black conservative agenda and was doing his best to teach me there are multiple ways to define myself as a Black male. Like my friends, I sagged my pants not because I saw it as a form of political resistance, but because my favorite artist, Tupac wore his pants that way. My father's examples of graduating from college impressed upon me I was capable of doing well in school, but our lack of ability to have intimate conversations pushed me to find other ways for validation.

Within schools and families are opportunities to influence masculinity constructs among Black boys. It is important to challenge the performance of hyper-masculine behaviors because they can lead to violence, academic underachievement, and other dangerous consequences. Through dialogue and demonstration educators and parents can engage Black males in meaningful activities that can expand the dominant perspectives that often influence self-destructive behaviors. Such activities that allow for conversations and growth to take place can take place in an array of creative extracurricular or co-curricular activities.

I believe it is possible to create safe spaces within schools and homes to encourage Black males to re-define thug. There is research to support the effectiveness of after-school programs to help Black males achieve their full potential (Clark, Harris, White-Smith, Allen, & Ray, 2010; Zimmerman,

Eisman, & Reischi, 2017; Noguera, 2003). In working with Black males, I have found the use of the communal philosophies, rituals, music, dance, acrobatic, and self-defense movements of the African-Brazilian called Capoeira to serve as a useful engagement tool. Through conversations and the planning of direct actions, I have found Capoeira effective to complement culturally relevant curricula and to explore the necessary self-knowledge to create positive changes within the Black community. There are activities that schools and families can engage to reinforce Black males as valuable assets in resistance movements aimed to resist racial injustices and address social inequalities.

The impact of racism upon communities of color has created a consensus among many males of color that life is "a survival of the fittest." To be fit as a Black boy means you must seek validation through your physical display of strength, clothing, attitude, and any other methods of communication consistent with socially constructed masculine behavior. The story presented in this chapter exemplifies how this came to fruition in my life. In spite of the necessity to teach Black boys to survive within their environment, it is also important that we encourage vulnerability. We must help Black boys to discover positive self-awareness, which includes actively engaging an authentic version of themselves to strive for their full potential.

When we downplay the significance of expressing the full range of emotions that we possess, the outcomes can lead to poor decisions with dire consequences. For Black boys, the suppression of emotions can lead to violent outbursts, academic underachievement, and other behaviors that can lead to prison, dropping out of school, or in some cases death. Jawanza Kunjufu (2005) claims that too often Black boys learn from a young age they must resolve conflicts through fighting; my transition to the suburbs confirms this aspect of his argument. If it weren't for my parents' persistence in keeping me in church, extracurricular activities and among men who challenged the societal pull toward self-destructive choices, I would not have achieved the level of academic success I have today.

Hip-Hop can be a viable tool when working with Black males because it can be used to inspire a new understanding of masculinity alongside social and political consciousness. While Tupac's music was not perfect and in some ways upheld many of the behaviors that often bear negative consequences for Black males, his artistic contributions reflect the potential of Hip Hop music. As Mychal Denzel Smith (2016) proclaimed in his book, *Invisible World Got the Whole World Watching; A Young Black Man's Education*, Tupac was a political figure who expressed the rage of a generation. Other artists who have created similar content to Tupac following his premature death, include J Cole, Kendrick Lamar, Talib Kweli, Common, Yasiin Bey, The Roots, and Lupe Fiasco. Like Tupac, the entire span of their music is not positive and reflective of the potential to raise awareness and redefine masculinity for Black males. However, I believe these artists and other representations within Hip-Hop can encourage a productive dialogue between adults and Black boys about race, racism, and masculinity.

As an educator, I have used my experiences with Hip-Hop as described in this chapter to encourage critical conversations with young Black males. Our dialogues begin with the mutual understanding that Hip-Hop serves as a valuable tool to magnify the voices and experiences of Black males. These youth-focused discussions allowed for honest and open talks about the indications of Black male identity in America. Among some of the young Black men who I have mentored, these discussions have led to changes in their behavior and academic performances.

In this chapter's narrative, I illustrate how I severely struggled with the performance of masculinity to make friends. Although my parents told me that I possessed the skills of a leader, I refused to accept that role. It was easier to follow my friends and seek status through poor relationships with girls, defiance of school policies, and an average approach to academics. I began to think differently about school after a series of events that led to a suspension in high school.

To download the FREE PDF workbook and instructional guide, please visit: www.vlindsayphd.com/crtblackmales

References

Chang, J. (2007). *Can't stop won't stop: A history of the hip-hop generation.* New York, NY: St. Martin's Press.

Clark, R., Harris, A., White-Smith, A. K., Allen, R. W., & Ray, B. A. (2010). The positive effects of after-school programs for African American Male Development and Educational Progress. In E. W. Johnson Jr. (Ed.), *Social work with African American males* (pp. 117–147). New York, NY: Oxford University Press.

Coates, T. (2017). *We Were Eight Years in Power: An American Tragedy.* New York, NY: One World/Ballantine.

Dyson, M. E. (2005). *Is Bill Cosby Right?: Or Has the Black Middle Class Lost Its Mind?.* New York, NY: Civitas Books.

Hutchinson, E. O. (2006). *The assassination of the black male image.* New York, NY: Touchstone.

Jeffries, D., & Jeffries, R. (2017). Marxist Materialism and Critical Race Theory: A Comparative Analysis of Media and Cultural Influence on the Formation of Stereotypes and Proliferation of Police Brutality against Black Men. *Spectrum: A Journal on Black Men, 5*(2), 1–22.

Kunjufu, J. (2005). *Countering the conspiracy to destroy Black boys.* Chicago, IL: African American Images.

Noguera, P. A. (2003). The trouble with Black boys: The role and influence of environmental and cultural factors on the academic performance of African American males. *Urban education, 38*(4), 431–459.

Smith, D. M. (2016). *Invisible man got the whole world watching: A young Black man's education.* New York, NY: Nation Books.

Travis, R. (2013). Rap music and the empowerment of today's youth: Evidence in everyday music listening, music therapy, and commercial rap music. *Child and Adolescent Social Work Journal, 30*(2), 139–167.

Zimmerman, M. A., Eisman, A. B., Reischl, T. M., Morrel-Samuels, S., Stoddard, S., Miller, A. L., Hutchnison, P., Franzen, S., & Rupp, L. (2017). Youth Empowerment Solutions: Evaluation of an after-school program to engage middle school students in community change. *Health Education & Behavior, 45* (1), 20–31.

· 4 ·

FOLLOW THE LEADER

Introduction

Despite some of the challenges I encountered during middle and junior high school, I made it to high school. I attended Thornwood High School in South Holland which was about twelve blocks from my parents' home. When I began high school, the environment appeared diverse like my junior high school with regards to racial representations across the student body. By the time, I reached my junior year "White flight," the unlikely coincidence that some White families decide to move when communities become increasingly diverse, was in full effect. The majority of the students who attended Thornwood High School at the time I became an upperclassman were Black and part of a dramatic shift in the school culture that impacted school policies.

Following the 1999 school shooting at Columbine High School in Littleton, Colorado, my high school responded to the perceived fears of violence with new measures to increase safety. Among the revised policies, there was a mandate issued that all students and staff wear the school issued identification cards on a lanyard around their neck while on campus. School administrators believed this was the best method to secure the facility from armed students with the potential to repeat the actions of the Columbine shooters.

Without remote intention to follow in the footsteps of the Colorado students, I refused to wear the ID card, and earned an in-school suspension.

Due to my past experiences in K-8 schools, I developed an allergy to the words compliance and authority. As a young Black male who often felt excluded from curriculum, I did not hold a great respect for my teachers or the institution that claimed to provide an education. Although I didn't call me or my peers' desperate association with sports as athlete seasoning complex (Edwards, 2000; Eitle & Eitle, 2002; Harris, 2012; Howard, 2014), I searched for self-validation through sports activity, the pursuit of money and girls rather than leadership and strong academics. My parents told me to appreciate school and that my friends would continue to admire me, but I just wanted to be one of the guys. As a teenager, there were many moments when I did not value myself or school.

My parents and other adults tried to get me to understand the importance of leadership in high school. Dad taught me leadership is the act of creating a plan others will follow. Mom taught me leadership means committing to a goal and following-through with the difficult process to ensure it happens. My teachers taught that a leader is an individual who makes decisions, despite the criticism they may receive from others. Every adult in my life tried to get me to understand the value in creating a positive influence in my community and among my friends. In high school, I was not ready.

Follow the Leader

When I began high school, it had been a long time since I heard my kindergarten teachers say the phrase "follow the leader." These three words, follow the leader, were often whispered and occasionally yelled at me whenever I was out of the single file line or refused to hold my partner's hand. Leaders were students who did everything right. From a young age, I accepted the limiting belief that seeking recognition as the leader was not the desired goal for other Black boys and me.

I can still remember the day my mother dropped me off for my first day of high school at Thornwood High School. We pulled out of the driveway in her gray 1982 Volvo sedan listening to her favorite conservative Christian radio channel. One of the songs she enjoyed was on the air as we pulled out of the driveway and she began to sing while driving down the street.

I was not interested in talking with her on that morning because I had a feeling she would lecture me about making wise choices in high school and staying out of trouble. As a teenager, there was nothing she could tell me about my life because I believed her advice was outdated and designed to prevent me from having a good time. The suggestions she often offered me were based on her experiences, which I thought were ancient and disconnected from my reality.

I could not visualize my mother as a teenager who shared similar experiences with me. She was 42 years old, which, at the time, I thought was extremely old. My mother grew up without cell phones, the internet, and many other modern tools of communication and convenience. I thought it was impossible for her to understand me as a fourteen-year-old Black male. We were indeed from different generations, but that was not going to stop her from trying to give me some advice.

The song on the radio ended as we arrived at the corner of 170th Street, and I cringed. I anticipated "the talk" about her high school experiences, which I was convinced occurred during the same time dinosaurs roamed the earth! The first day of high school was a significant day that represented one more step toward adulthood, so I knew my mom would not allow it to pass without offering me some advice or encouragement.

As we passed the junior high school I attended, she decided to speak. The conversation began with an annoying parental question. "Vernon, do you know that you are a leader?" My parents liked to remind me that I was a leader, before each moment that I was away from their direct supervision. It was an indirect way of telling me to behave like I had some sense. I didn't respond to my mother's question, but I looked at her out of the corner of my eye, trying to determine the words that might quell her concerns about me starting high school.

She continued before I could get a word out of my mouth. "It's obvious to me that you are a leader. I've seen the way your friends admire and respect you." I nodded yes, but didn't agree with her comments. It was clear to me my friends often decided to help whenever I needed something, but I dismissed it as evidence that I was a leader within my crew.

My mother continued: "You've got to live up to your potential. Don't worry about trying to impress your friends. As I said before, they already admire you. So just be yourself and don't forget what me and your father taught you at home. Forget about this Yellow Monkey stuff. You're a handsome young man, and the girls will always be there. Take your education seriously, and be willing to make the difficult, but right, decisions in and out of school." The commands that began our conversation were merely the prelude to more advice she would offer me in the brief ride to my first day of high school.

Anytime there was mention of girls in my vicinity who were not my sisters, my mother reminded me of the importance in demonstrating respect. "Don't be mannish," is what she said to me as we pulled into the parking lot at Thornwood. It was her way of telling me to focus on education and not girlfriends. I was a freshman in a high school with students from several local communities. My mother knew there would be plenty of new pretty faces and she wanted me to remember that I was there to learn.

The conversation ended with her telling me about how quickly the four years of high school would pass. With the intention to motivate, she said to me that I was a freshman, but one day soon it would be time for me to graduate and attend college like my older sisters. As I began to open the car door and walk towards high school, my mother grabbed my hand. She looked me firmly in my eyes and sang, "remember that only what you do for Christ matters."

I received her message, but I was unable to respond. My mother knew I needed to make some adjustments in my thinking to realize my potential and be successful in high school. It was clear to her that I valued the opinions of my friends and occasionally made poor decisions to impress them. She wanted me to resist the temptation of being like everyone else and to instead carve my path down a road that led to positive choices and actions in the world. It was clear to me that she perceived me as a leader who my friends and others should follow.

My mom wanted to ensure I became a Black man who made choices with the right type of mindset. She believed in my potential to be a great leader but thought I needed to shift the perspectives I had of the world and myself for it to be realized. I didn't value growth or understand how failing at anything did not make me also a failure. Mom wanted me to learn from my past mistakes to make more productive and positive choices in the future. When I began high school, I didn't find value in the courage to reach for excellence in every area of my life.

My parents had much more faith in my leadership skills than I did when I started high school. On the morning my mom dropped me off at Thornwood's main entrance, I was more concerned about other things I believed were more important than making good choices. The questions I asked myself included: Should I have ironed my shirt this morning? Will I need to fight on my first day? What are the girls going to be like? Where is my homeroom class? Will there be any cute girls in my homeroom? Where are my friends? Did they take all the girls? Will I need to make new friends? The idea of reflecting the positive values of my household were simply not on my radar as I began high school.

Thornwood High School was where I would spend four crucial years of my life. I was pessimistic they would begin on a positive note because my sisters had forwarned me of a hazing tradition involving upperclassmen and first-year students. With this fear in mind, I was convinced that I would have to fight someone who was interested in keeping the practice of bullying freshmen students alive. Carrying over from fifth grade, I was not afraid to fight and willing to confront anyone who threatened my wellbeing for the sake of status.

As my mom drove away in her Volvo, I walked toward the entrance of the school with my class schedule in hand. I hoped that as soon as I opened the door, I would be able to find some friends from my previous school to look for our homerooms together. We talked about meeting near the main entrance of Thornwood to walk in as a group in case upperclassmen ambushed us, but I did not see anyone familiar as I approached the main doors for students and visitors.

Walking into the school, the first thing I noticed was the security desk with two uniformed officers who sat and stared in my direction. They took one look at me, and I could see the wheels being turned by individual and systemic racism in their head. Their thoughts ran together, and I imagined they included: "here's another uneducated Black male; he will get suspended; I wonder if he will graduate; I will be the one to arrest him." One of the officers said aloud, "all the freshmen homerooms reside on the first floor. You have six minutes to locate your class, so I would get a move on it and not walk so slow."

As I passed the security desk, I looked back in their direction and said with a smirk, "thanks." I walked an additional thirty steps before I made a right turn and proceeded up the stairs. The security officer told me all freshmen homerooms were on the first floor, but I wanted to explore the campus and find my friends. My mom said leadership is about making difficult decisions, and I decided not to follow the security officer's suggestions.

As I walked to find my friends instead of my homeroom, I was intimidated by what I saw on the staircase and in the hallway that led to the second floor of the school. Some boys were twice my size and had fully grown beards! I thought about my mother's words of living up to my potential, as I passed boys who were similar in height and build to the men in my life. My mom forgot to tell me about the grown men who posed as students in high school. I thought that if any one of these guys attempted to fight me, I was out of my league in size and strength.

Once I reached the top of the stairs, I looked to my left and right for any of the guys who I would later collectively call *FAAM*. I searched for anyone from my junior high school, but I quickly became lost in a wilderness full of strange faces. There were so many students that it felt impossible to find any of my friends. I did see several girls who I thought were pretty, but I lacked the confidence to do anything other than smile.

My friends and I were not leaders in the relationships we pursued with girls. "Pimp or Die" was the motto that we claimed to live, yet we were often fearful of merely initiating contact with the opposite sex. We were not pimps by any stretch of the imagination and knew nothing about exploiting women for money and selling their bodies for sex. Pimping within my circle of friends mostly meant that we maintained the attention of as many girls as possible. I wasn't bold enough to be honest about the number of girls who were actually in my life, so instead of acting like a leader who did things differently in our group, I lied. My friends and I were frequently not honest among ourselves and in our relationships with girls, but we were not pimps.

At the top of the staircase, I looked and smiled at many girls in search of a familiar face from junior high. I did not talk to any of them, but I admired their beauty and wished I dared to introduce myself. There were a few who smiled in my direction, but they did not say anything to me. It was an unspoken rule, that, as the male, I was supposed to initiate contact. That was not going to happen at this specific moment, so only an occasional smile was exchanged as they walked pass me in the hallway. As I stood in that massive hallway and looked at all the girls who I was too afraid to approach, I lost track of time and my surroundings.

I did not notice that as I stood there gawking at the girls, someone approached me from behind. "Yellow Monkey you are supposed to be on the first floor!" It was my sister, Erica who was a senior in high school. "Shut-up you loser, I'm looking for one of my friends." She laughed and then warned me if I were caught by one of the deans after the bell rang, I would be issued a detention on the first day of school.

I had my fair share of detentions in junior high, and they were not pleasant experiences. Detentions in junior high school involved sitting after school for an hour in complete silence or coming to school on a Saturday and cleaning the classrooms for three hours. I couldn't imagine the type of torture they put students through in high school, so I decided to turn around and locate my homeroom. I believed that at least one of my friends from junior high might be in the same homeroom or I might run into someone on the way to the classroom.

At this point, I had two minutes to get my bearings and locate the classroom before the tardy bell was scheduled to ring. My pace changed from a casual walk to a slight jog and eventually became a full out sprint. One teacher called out after me, "Young man, walk in the hallway!" I ignored her and continued to run in the direction of where I believed the classroom was located. Just as the bell began to ring, I arrived at the homeroom that I thought was correct.

The teacher was standing at the door and as I arrived she greeted me with a smile. I returned the gesture and walked inside the classroom to take a seat. As soon I located the first available seat, I sat down and attempted to control my breathing. I didn't want to bring any additional attention to myself by using my asthma inhaler in the classroom, so I took long and deep breaths to cool down.

As soon as I gained my composure, I put my head up and began to take a look around the classroom. There were White, Black, Asian, and Latino/a students in my homeroom, and I didn't recognize any of their faces. I was the only one from my junior high school, and everyone looked much older than me. At my previous school, I had a significant number of friends who I considered second to family, FAAM, but none of them were in this classroom. I was scared that I would have to start from scratch with making new friends.

Attendance was the first item on her agenda for that day and the teacher, Ms. Fisher, began to read names from her roster in alphabetical order. I listened for my name as she traveled through the list of students who responded with "here" when they heard their name called. Ms. Fisher made it all the way through the class roster to the last name on the list, which was Zornell. She never called my name. "Is there anyone's name I didn't call," Ms. Fisher asked. I reluctantly put my hand in the air as I pulled out the wrinkled piece of paper from my pocket with the schedule.

I reread the numbers next to homeroom on my printed schedule and realized I was in the wrong classroom! My schedule indicated 114, and I was in room 112. In the process of rushing to beat the bell and avoid the detention my sister warned me of, I went into the wrong classroom. This mistake was incredibly embarrassing as a freshman student who was trying to make a positive first impression with an intention to make more friends.

I slowly stood up and walked to Ms. Fisher to show her my schedule. She responded with kindness and patience. "Mistakes happen, and it is your first day. The classroom you belong in is right next door, and I can walk with you to excuse your tardy." I could hear students in the classroom giggle, and a few whispered, "freshman." I didn't want to face them, so I turned toward the door and kept my eyes focused in front of me as I left the classroom.

Ms. Fisher and I turned right as we reached the hallway and knocked on the door to room 112. We were greeted by my assigned homeroom teacher, Mr. Schultz. I took five steps into the classroom, and then I heard a familiar voice say, "Vern-Dawg."

It was my friend Sam. We attended the same junior high school, and I was surprised to see him sitting in the back row of the classroom. I talked to him a few days prior, but we did not discuss our homeroom assignments. After seeing him, I was relieved from the anxiety of having to meet new friends. I nodded my head in his direction and found a seat next to him.

Sam was a close friend of mine, and I was thrilled to see that we were in the same homeroom. He was the comedian of my crew and a great person to be around. As I took my seat, I knew as soon as Mr. Schultz found out we were friends, I would have to find another desk. I tried to be discreet, but I knew it would not be long before we were discovered.

Sam turned to me and said, "Why were you late on the first day of school, man?" For a moment it crossed my mind that it would be best to ignore him, but I decided to respond. "I wasn't. I just went to the wrong classroom." Sam laughed. "Oh, you can't read, freshman!"

"Yes, I can read, fool. I was just rushing and went into the wrong classroom. I knew I was assigned 112 as my homeroom, but I was rushing to avoid getting a tardy slip on the first day. It didn't dawn on me until after the teacher next door went through her attendance roster, that I was in the wrong classroom."

Sam didn't buy my explanation. "The Yellow Monkey who can't read!"

I laughed, said "shut-up whore," and Mr. Schultz looked directly in my direction. My efforts to be discreet about my friendship with Sam lasted all of sixty seconds; it was clear to everyone, including Mr. Schultz, that we were friends and should not sit next to each other.

Mr. Schultz said, "Vernon is your name, right?" When I confirmed my name, he continued. "I realize that you are a freshman student and you do not understand the ins and outs of high school quite yet. That language is inappropriate, and this is not the time to talk. It is clear to me that you are friends with the person next to you and I need to find you a new seat. Please take the seat that is available in the first row."

There went my first impression with my homeroom teacher. I looked at Sam to indicate it was his fault I was being punished. He smiled at me and then pointed in the direction of my newly assigned seat. He was getting a thrill out of seeing me disciplined in front of a classroom of thirty students. I was embarrassed, so I gathered my things while keeping my head down and with my coolest stroll walked to the front row. It was not my goal to get called out in front of my peers and get ordered to sit in the front row like a teacher's pet. That was precisely what I did not want as my first impression with my homeroom teacher or classmates.

After I sat down, Mr. Schultz began to speak to the class. "Welcome to your first day of high school! I will be serving as your homeroom teacher for your freshman year and assist you to make a successful transition from junior high to high school. After we take attendance, I will offer you some advice that I believe will help you to do your best in any class here at Thornwood."

Mr. Schultz quickly read through the names of the students in the class. It was clear to me by the speed at which he read the names; this was the second time he checked attendance, and I was the only one that needed verification. Immediately after finishing the roster, Mr. Schultz began his introductory to high school lecture. "Excellent, now that we have completed attendance, I want to provide you with five classroom practices that will help you to produce your best work in any class. Please take out a notebook and a writing utensil."

I opened my book bag, grabbed my notebook, and an ink pen to write down Mr. Schultz's recommendations for classroom success. He talked for nearly forty-five minutes without a pause. The most important suggestion that stayed with me was to search for connections between the lessons in the classroom and your life. He emphasized that if we can find a way to identify with the material, it would resonate better with us, increase learning in the subject, and improve our chances of earning good grades. Mr. Schultz also talked about the importance of sitting upright and reflecting open body language toward the teacher and materials.

I wrote down the advice of Mr. Schultz, but initially, I did not think once about applying it in my approach toward school. The behaviors I embraced up until this point appeared to be working just fine for me. My posture in class conveyed an attitude of fatigue and boredom; I frequently sat sluggishly in my chair with my arms crossed in front of my chest. I was rarely intrigued by what the teacher had to offer or asked questions in class. The teacher's lesson plans always took second place to talk with my friends during class. In most of my classes, I only learned the material for the sake of an effort to get decent grades or to score well on a test. I infrequently saw connections between school and my life, but somehow I passed each class and made it to high school.

I decided to resume my behavior practices from my K-8 schools and ignore Mr. Schultz's advice. His comments about connecting the teacher's lesson and conveying open body language resonated with me, because I often felt bored in class and showed it via facial expressions or by putting my head down. Although I wrote down what he had to offer, I was hesitant to apply it in my classes. However, every time I got in trouble in school or I reached the end of a quarter and was disappointed with my grades, I thought about the advice Mr. Schultz provided me on my first day of high school.

By the time, I reached my junior year in high school I somehow managed to earn average grades in many of my classes. For fear of looking lame to my peers, but not wanting to get in trouble at home with my parents, I intentionally only did what was necessary to pass my classes. A part of me knew that school was important, but it took a back seat to the social activities that drove this phase of my life. Despite my efforts to sabotage my grades, at the end of several quarters, I earned an "A" or "B" in some of my classes. The potential was in me, but I had a hard time acknowledging my abilities, and I held on to a strong disdain for persons in authoritative roles who enforced school policies.

With each year I attended high school, there appeared to be more restrictions placed on students. Policies were continually revised and adjusted, as the school culture of Thornwood High School began to change. One school policy that I notably did not like was the requirement for all students to wear their identification (ID) cards around their neck on a lanyard at all times while on school property. In addition to students, teachers and administrators were required to wear their ID cards as part of the revised policy during my junior year. If you were a visitor, the security personnel provided you with an adhesive name tag you had to stick to your clothes. Everyone in the school was required to wear visible identification.

The Columbine school shooting was one incident that had an impact on the implementation of the new school policies. On April 20, 1999, Eric Harris and Dylan Klebold, killed thirteen students and injured twenty-one others including teachers and staff. Many schools, including Thornwood, responded to this act of violence with policies predicated on beliefs that school violence was on the rise and such measures such as mandatory ID policies would increase safety (Altheide, 2009; Lewis, 2003; Tuchman, 1999). In addition to the impact of Columbine, the racial demographics of Thornwood high school significantly changed from the time I was a freshman until my junior year in high school.

When my mother dropped me off on my first day at Thornwood, the student population was reasonably diverse across representations of racial groups. However, with each year the diversity diminished and it became a school where the majority students in attendance racially identified as Black and ethnically as African American. This change in student demographics supported the implementation of racialized policies motivated by beliefs of criminalization and academic underachievement. There were community concerns that I gleaned from my parents' involvement in the neighborhood that students of color were lowering the value of education in the district.

In a memo sent home, the school indicated that the ID policy was a measure to increase school safety, security, and to prepare students for future employment opportunities. My peers and I saw the policy as a tool of control; it indicated that when we entered our high school's doors, we released our identities and became another piece of property that belonged to the school. As a student with growing popularity, I saw the ID as an accessory that interfered with my ability to attract girls. I was concerned that wearing the ID on the blue lanyard made me look lame and in compliance with the school's rules.

I was primarily in school to get girlfriends, hang out with my friends, and then obtain an education. That was the order of my priorities, and any school policy that I believed conflicted with these priorities was resisted with full force. I was one of many students who would keep the ID card in their pocket and only show it when asked by a teacher. This subtle act of resistance gained me respect among my friends and notoriety with teachers and administrators.

On one day in my junior year of high school, Ms. Washington, my history teacher who was a White woman, became infuriated with my complete defiance of the school ID policy. In her class on American history where I frequently arrived late and placed my ID around my neck as I found my seat, we rarely discussed any of the positive contributions that African people made to society. When we were not passively listening about Europe and its descendants in North America, she primarily focused on maintaining control of the class. We were not allowed to talk or stand to throw anything in the trash without her permission; if we chose to violate her rules, a detention was imminent. It was clear to me I was not her favorite student, and my disregard for the school ID policy furthered her disdain for my behavior.

Ms. Washington made a note of the number of occasions throughout several weeks where multiple teachers asked me to wear my ID card, and I did not comply with their requests. I had no choice but to wear my ID in her class, but as soon as I left it returned to the pocket of my jeans. Unbeknownst to me, she took meticulous notes on how I often took my ID out of my pocket upon request, but as soon as a teacher was out of sight, I put it away. Ms. Washington kept a tally of the violations that she witnessed and waited for the perfect opportunity to recommend a suspension to my assigned school dean.

The moment for Ms. Washington came on a day when I was walking down the hallway with my arm around a girl I was desperately trying to impress. I was caught up whispering something flirtatious and failed to notice that I was directly in front of Ms. Washington's class. In the weeks prior, Ms. Washington had become quite a nuisance in her persistence of me wearing the ID card. Whenever I attended her class or walked pass her door, I tried my best to remember that she was an enforcer of the policy I despised. While I was busy in romantic bliss, Ms. Washington was grabbing the referral forms to send me to the dean.

As soon as I reached the door to her classroom, she said, "Vernon, I am tired of asking you to wear your ID card. This policy requires mandatory compliance, and you are not exempt from adherence." I started to pull my ID card out of my pocket. Ms. Washington stopped me and said, "It's too late."

She went on to explain. "I have observed you violate this policy on multiple occasions, and I am going to send your dean a referral for suspension. You pretend that you will place it around your neck, and then as soon as a teacher or administrator turns their head you put it back in your pocket."

I thought to myself that there is no way I can escape this one. Ms. Washington had well documented my act of resistance against the school policy. She did not care about my motives to not conform to the demands of others with the intention to maintain a sense of my identity. In her eyes my decision not to wear the ID card was not an act of protest against a misguided and racially justified policy. Ms. Washington saw me as a Black male who was defiant and disrespectful toward other adults in the building. As she handed me the referral slip, she ordered me to go to the dean's office and explain to him why I believed the school should grant me exemption status to the security policy that required all students and staff to wear identification cards.

By the time I reached the dean's office he had already spoken with Ms. Washington. They talked on the phone and agreed that an in-school suspension was a suitable punishment. I didn't have a chance to explain myself. Ms. Washington's referral documented three separate violations of the school identification policy. My dean, an older White man, had zero tolerance for any violation of school policies. He authorized the suspension immediately and then told me to remain in the dean's office for the rest of the school day.

On the following morning, I was assigned to remain in a classroom in an isolated part of the school building with other suspended Black male students. In my mind, high school felt like a prison. The ID cards were equivalent to the numbers assigned to inmates at their time of admittance. Teachers and administrators observed my every move, and so I likened them to correctional officers. Ann Arnett Ferguson (2000) argues that schools can serve as vehicles to punish Black males and transport them directly to the prison system. As I sat in the suspension room, these prison comparisons surfaced, and I believed that I was placed in separation from the general population.

One of the uniformed security officers whom I swore convicted me on my first day as a freshman student, told us we would spend the entire day in silence. If our teachers decided to send us homework, we were permitted to work on the assignments. In the event they did not, which was my case, we were told to quietly sit and stare at the wall in front of us. We were not allowed to sleep or talk to other students. If we decided to violate any of these rules, they told us we would earn a suspension for two additional days.

While in suspension, I had a lot of time to think about the decisions that put me in that predicament. I was upset with Ms. Washington and the dean who authorized the in-school suspension. I was upset with myself for not having the foresight to know Ms. Washington would be watching my every move. My previous interactions taught me that she would not attempt to understand it as an act of resistance with implications about the school's policy. The in-school suspension did not encourage me to change my behavior; rather, it fueled my anger.

After my release from the in-school suspension room to probation among my peers, I was informed that I needed to meet with my counselor before returning to class. I did not understand the purpose of the meeting because I did not have a relationship with my counselor. We saw each other four times a year, at the start of each quarter when it was time for me to register for classes. That was the only service I believed he provided. My counselor was a middle age White man named Mr. Smith, and I knew he could not offer a solution to the resentment I felt toward the school.

Mr. Smith did not experience my conviction from the security officers on the day I walked through the doors of Thornwood High School as a freshman student. He did not know how it felt to be in classes as a young Black boy and only learn about Black people's contributions to society as slaves and pacifists in the civil rights era. My counselor did not know what it felt like to attend a school where teachers' expectations changed when the White students went on an exodus known as "White flight," because suddenly there were too many people of color in their neighborhood.

With the understanding that the counselor and I did not have anything in common, I was not open to a meeting after the suspension. Regardless of my feelings, I did not have a choice in the decision to have the meeting with Mr. Smith. The follow-up counseling session was the standard protocol for all students returning from suspension. This policy was an additional measure taken by the school to determine if a student was ready to return to class.

Mr. Smith began our counseling session asking for an account of the events that led to the suspension. I didn't believe he would listen, but I reluctantly complied with the request. Mr. Smith sat quietly without interruption, while looking at a set of files in a manila folder; it was clear to me that he prematurely assessed me and the situation. As soon as I finished explaining my perspective, he took a moment to write down some notes and then formed his response.

His comments were part of what shifted my approach toward education. He began the conversation by asking me about my plans after high school. I told him that I planned to attend a university and major in business. He took one look at me and then referenced my record of detentions, average grades, and my recent release from suspension to suggest that I was out of touch with reality. Mr. Smith replied, "Vernon, I think you should take a look at the local junior college. That would be your best bet."

It was clear to me that he only saw me as a young Black male who did not have the potential to pursue a four-year degree. He did not believe I was capable of meeting the academic or social standards to attend a university and the pursuit of an Associate degree was the safer route. I knew his recommendation was not based on sound financial advice that encouraged the completion of general education requirements at a junior college before proceeding to a university. Instead, it was derived from his perception of my race, gender, behavior in school, and the belief that I did not have the potential to earn a degree from a university.

My high school counselor did not see or care to recognize that systemic and individual racism were factors that influenced my performances in school. Mr. Smith didn't understand it was difficult for me to perform well on standardized tests that were culturaly biased. It wasn't important to him, teachers, or other staff members that I learned about people who looked like me in class. Irrelevant to his assumptions about my potential was the fact that from the third grade on I felt like people in schools prematurely labeled me as deficient. He reduced my experiences with race to work ethic and behavior.

Mr. Smith's comments made me upset, but they were the necessary fuel to ignite a different approach to school. For the remainder of the school year, I arrived determined to get better grades in my classes and gain admittance to a university. While I remained committed to wearing my ID card only when necessary, I decided that it was no longer cool to focus primarily on relationships with girls and sacrifice my education in the process. It was still vital for me to have a girlfriend, but it also became imperative for me to do well in school.

I began to understand the reality of race and racism as motivational tools for success. As a Black male, I was fully aware that others would doubt my ability to do well in life. My earlier experiences going back to the third grade and the trip to Florida were the predecessors to this interaction with my high school counselor. Instead of ignoring race, I embraced it and began to use it as a tool to enable perseverance when I experienced challenges. I realized it would take more than just working hard, being disciplined, and embracing leadership to accomplish my goals in school. It would require a belief in myself, a push beyond the impossible, and the awareness that racism exists to ultimately lead me to the success I wanted for my life.

With this new understanding that did not develop overnight, I began to reconsider the advice my mother and Mr. Schultz offered me on the first day of school. When I returned from suspension, a friend of mine recommended me to check out the music of *Dead Prez*. They were a Hip-Hop duo, M-1 and Sticman, who created politically and socially conscious music. Listening to tracks like, "They School" and "I'm a African" inspired me to learn more about my history and recognize that I had the leadership potential my mother aimed to make me realize. I began to believe that if I followed Mr. Schultz's advice that I could liberate myself and help others through education.

In time, my perspective of academic achievement evolved, and I avoided side conversations with my peers. When I sat in my seat, I no longer sat sluggishly and conveyed complete disinterest in the subject. I asked questions, looked for ways to make connections between the curriculum and my life, and completed my homework on time. This new approach toward school was not an overnight process, but gradual steps taken to ensure I maximized the possibility of being admitted to a university.

My friends noticed the difference in my behavior as well and began to look at me as a leader. Despite my change in approach toward academics, I remained friends with Sam and other friends; throughout high school we listened to the same music, and continued to lie to each other about the number of girls in our lives. The difference came in how I spent my time studying and completing homework, in addition to the new conversations I had about attending college. When I graduated from high school, I no longer resented the idea of recognition as a leader, but due to the culmination of my K-12 experiences, I remained underprepared for college.

What does this story indicate is the potential for Black males to influence school culture and school policies?

In my dissertation (Lindsay, 2013), I discuss the use of extracurricular programs to engage Black males in transformative resistance to impact school cultures and school policies. The work is a snapshot from a larger four-year research study that explored the experiences of a cohort of young Black males enrolled in an urban high school. I found value in a culturally relevant after-school curriculum, a stomp team that was organized by an administrator, and other activities as mentioned in the previous chapter, Capoeira, to be effective tools to mentor and encourage academic achievement among young Black males. A key finding of the research was that it is possible to make meaning of the resistance behaviors some Black males engage in high school.

This chapter discusses my experiences in high school and the attempts to not comply with the success strategies offered to me by my mother and teachers. It talked about my obsession with girls and the suspension I endured for refusal to adhere to the ID policy. During high school, I was not involved in any activities that could have potentially rechanneled my negative resistance behaviors into something positive. Although not discussed within this narrative, it is important to note that I didn't play organized sports and as soon as I reached the legal age to work, I found a job to afford dates with girls. In high school, my priorities included dating and hanging out with my friends; academics were secondary.

The decision to not wear my ID was prompted by a change in the school culture and school policies that I believe were influenced by the Columbine high school shooting and the shift in student racial demographics. Thornwood responded to the Columbine shooting like many schools throughout the United States with revised policies geared toward the perception of creating a safer environment. The change in school policy also came at a time when the

students of color became the overwhelming majority in a school that historically educated young people who identified as White. I felt the change in my
high school's culture, and it encouraged me to resist.

After being readmitted to school after a suspension for insubordination,
my counselor's comments confirmed that many of my high school teachers
and administrators' expectations were lowered due to racially biased assumptions of me and my peers' potential. I was told by my high school counselor
that the local junior college was a more appropriate fit for me after graduation.
His advice was not based on a strategy to save my family money; it was because
he believed that I was unprepared to be successful in a four-year university setting. My counselor's comments were reflective of dismissing the intersections
between racism and masculinity constructs.

Educators and administrators of Black males have an opportunity to
improve their schools when they decide to disect behaviors that are often prejudged as merely defiant. I refused to wear the ID because I believed the policy
was created out of fear and it interfered with my ability to express my indi-
viduality. Other acts of resistance can be teachable if we allow the voices of
Black males to be heard in high school. Instead of suspending students where
they are taken away from instruction, it is possible to engage in meaningful
dialogue that can lead to improvements in school policies and school cultures.
We can encourage Black males in the direction of positive leadership, if we
would listen to their experiences and be open to their perspectives.

As indicated in this narrative, I sat in a room and stared at a wall for an
entire day when I could have been provided with an opportunity to unpack
why I violated the policy. It is possible that I and the other Black males who
were suspended could have been instrumental in policies that quelled fears
of school violence. However, our suspension was nearly added to the significant number of Black males who as Jawanza Kunjufu (1990, 2005) claims are
often suspended for minor infractions. The only time I was allowed to explain
myself was after the suspension and in front of my counselor who had prematurely dismissed me as a young Black male with limited potential.

My high school counselor believed that because I was a young Black
male, who appeared disinterested in school I was not capable of a university.
His belief system that was influenced by his racial perception of my potential
informed him that I did not possess the skills to be successful beyond high
school. Mr. Smith stirred a desire in me to take a different approach toward
my education, and so I embraced what I believed were leadership skills for
success in the classroom. Unfortunately, my average grades coupled with my

poor performance on culturally biased standardized tests put me in a hole to get admitted to many universities. As I applied to colleges and received rejection letters, I began to wonder if the counselor was right.

To download the FREE PDF workbook and instructional guide, please visit: www.vlindsayphd.com/crtblackmales

References

Altheide, D. L. (2009). The Columbine shootings and the discourse of fear. *American Behavioral Scientist, 52*(10), 1354–1370.

Edwards, H. (2000). Crisis of black athletes on the eve of the 21st century. *Society, 37*(3), 9–13.

Eitle, T., & Eitle, D. (2002). Race, cultural capital, and the educational effects of participation in sports. *Sociology of Education, 75*, 123–146.

Ferguson, A. A. (2000). *Bad boys: Public schools in the making of black masculinity*. Ann Arbor, MI: University of Michigan Press.

Harris, P. C. (2012). The sports participation effect on educational attainment of Black males. *Education and Urban Society, 46* (5), 507–521.

Howard, T. C. (2014). *Black male (D): Peril and promise in the education of African American males*. New York, NY: Teachers College Press.

Kunjufu, J. (1990). *Countering the conspiracy to destroy black boys* (Vol. 3). Chicago, IL: African American Images.

Kunjufu, J. (2005). *Countering the conspiracy to destroy black boys*. Chicago, IL: African American Images.

Lewis, T. (2003). The surveillance of post-columbine schools. *Review of Education, Pedagogy and Cultural Studies Taylor and Francis, 25*(4), 335–355.

Lindsay, V. (2013). *"They Schools Ain't Teachin Us": Black males, resistance, and education at Uhuru High School* (Doctoral dissertation). Retrieved from Proquest database. University of Illinois at Chicago.

Tuchman, G. (1999). *Drills, new security measures mark return to schools*. CNN Retrieved on December 11, 2017 from http://edition.cnn.com/US/9908/16/school.safety/

· 5 ·

UNDERGRAD AND UNDERPREPARED

Introduction

When I started college, I was the fourth child in my immediate family to attend the University of Illinois at Chicago (UIC). Due to the cost of attendance, respectable reputation, and its' proximity to home, my sisters chose UIC for college. I decided to attend UIC because my high school transcript did not leave me with many options. Following the suspension discussed in the previous chapter I made some changes in my approach to school, but it was too late to override three years of poor study habits and limited extracurricular involvement. Thanks to an alternative admissions policy, UIC was the only option for me to attend a university directly after graduation.

Before beginning undergrad in the Fall semester of 2001, I believed that I left the intentional underperformance in academics in high school. I thought I was mentally prepared to be successful in college. In the first semester of my freshman year, I earned an "F" in intermediate algebra. The second time I took the course I earned a "D" which was enough to get exempt from the course, but not enough to earn credits toward graduation. In my sophomore, junior and senior years, I performed poorly on exams in other classes and did not always practice the necessary skills outside of the lecture halls to ensure I learned the material. Throughout the four years enrolled in college, there were courses I did exceptionally well in and others where I was happy to receive a passing grade at the end of the semester.

In high school, I did not perform well on standardized tests, so I developed a habit of rushing to get finished without putting forth much effort to accurately answer the questions. My poor American College Testing exam (ACT) scores are evidence of my challenges with regards to these types of exams. I was unaware of the research that supports the notion that cultural biases are laden in standardized tests (Fischer, 2004; Helms, 1992; Horsford & Grosland, 2013; Sólarzano & Yosso, 2016). The ACT just felt like another school thing without relevance to my life.

Regardless, of my feelings with regards to standardized tests, a high ACT score was one of the gold tickets for college admittance. I initially applied to UIC through the College of Business and was denied. My ACT scores and transcript that did not indicate high performance in math courses were used to justify the decision. Thankfully, the College of Liberal Arts and Sciences reevaluated my application and provided an opportunity to prove I could handle the demands of a university education.

Undergrad and Underprepared

There was a moment when I didn't know if I would attend college immediately after high school. I contemplated working for a year and sent out applications to only a few schools as a backup option. My parents' budget was already stretched due to their assistance with my older sisters' college tuitions, and so I decided only to apply to Illinois' schools. I didn't have any scholarships, so I had to rely on a combination of financial aid, my parents' income, and the part-time job I had to pay for school.

I applied to the College of Business at UIC because I wanted to be an entrepreneur. The type of business I desired to own one day was uncertain, but I believed going to college and obtaining the appropriate education was the first step. I did not research before applying to the College of Business to determine whether I met the criteria. To qualify for admission, applicants needed to possess an above average ACT score and a proven record of high academic achievement in math courses.

My high school transcripts illustrated significant academic progress between my freshman year and senior year in high school, but my cumulative grades and standardized test scores were average. I took the ACT twice, earning a composite score of sixteen in my first attempt and later a slight improvement to nineteen. The College of Business reviewed my transcript with low ACT exam scores and decided I was not a good fit for the program. They conveyed this information to me in a form letter sent to all applicants who were denied admittance to the college.

When I received the rejection letter I was deeply saddened and believed I would not go to a university after high school. I began to believe that my high school counselor, who told me to pursue a junior college education, was right about my inability to meet the academic load that came with admission to a university. These negative thoughts pushed me into a low area of my life where I suffered from regret and wished that I would have done things differently in high school. There was always a part of me that knew I was smart and could do well in high school but I could not make the connection between the curriculum and my life.

From the third grade through high school, I only remember learning about people of African descent during February as part of Black history month. When we learned about Black people, it was always in the context of slavery and the civil rights era. Dr. Martin Luther King Jr. and Rosa Parks were frequently the only faces shown me and my peers of our resistance movement. Malcolm X was often inaccurately depicted as a crazed lunatic who encouraged violence. Marcus Garvey, Nat Turner, Fammie Lo Hammer, Patrice Lumumba, Ella Baker, Angela Davis, Kwame Nkrumah, and Assata Shakur were among the champions who battled oppression and never met my schools' curricula.

About two weeks after I received my initial rejection letter from the College of Business, an additional letter from UIC arrived at my parents' doorstep. It came in a similar envelope to the one sent by the business college, so I believed it was a duplicate of the previous letter. I thought that to receive the same rejection letter twice was unreasonable torture, and I cursed as I walked toward the trash can to throw it out. Before closing the lid to the trash can, something told me to look at it again, and that's when I noticed the sender was different. It was from UIC, but from the College of Liberal Arts and Sciences and so I decided that it might be worth opening.

This letter began with the standard admissions' language, "after careful consideration of your application," and continued with offering me an opportunity to apply to the College of Liberal Arts and Sciences as an undeclared major. The letter indicated that although I did not meet the admission requirements for the business college, they would consider my application as part of their applicant pool. Reading this information gave me hope, I would have an opportunity to attend college at UIC so I decided to apply.

That second chance offered me was the first lesson in college that taught me how failure could open doors to second chances. After I received the initial rejection letter I convinced myself I would not attend college immediately after high school and instead work for a year. However, my parents encouraged me to reapply and not to accept the failure to get admitted on my first attempt as an indicator of whether I could be successful in college. I took their advice.

Within a week, I received a response from the College of Liberal Arts and Sciences. The letter indicated my application was approved for admission! I was excited and extremely grateful to have another opportunity to attend a university and prove my high school counselor wrong. At that moment, I believed I would prioritize my college education more than high school. I intended to do my best in every course that I took.

In the Fall of 2001, I began college at UIC, where I faced a terrible commute to campus that would range anywhere from one to two hours each way with traffic. I was still living at my parents' home in South Holland, and the traffic on the Bishop Forward and Dan Ryan expressways was utterly unpredictable. If it rained, snowed, or an accident occurred my travel time quickly doubled. While I was incredibly grateful to have the used car my parents bought me in the summer before college began, driving a manual shift vehicle in heavy traffic each day was tiresome and significantly impacted my attention span once I arrived at campus.

When I selected courses in my first semester, I did not consider the time required to commute to campus. I thought it was a good idea to get my classes finished as early as possible so I would have the remainder of the day to work, complete homework, and hang out with my friends. Maintaining at least a part-time job during college was mandatory for my siblings and me. My sisters and I had to work to assist with school expenses and to afford our social lives. When I scheduled my classes early in the day, I failed to think about time for transportation, leisure, and other responsibilities.

Due to my poor decisions, and the disconnect I felt between life and my K-12 schools, I did not have experience with creating a schedule that included study time. When thinking about my week, I only considered my class times and the hours I needed to be at my job. I did not know to include time to study, the commute to campus, my household responsibilities, and leisure time with my friends. From the first week of classes, it was pain-fully apparent I needed to make some adjustments in how I organized my schedule.

Attempting to arrive at UIC at 8 am for Math 090, *Intermediate Algebra*, was a nightmare. The traffic was horrendous, and if I made it on time for class, I was exhausted from the commute and found it difficult to concentrate on the professor's lectures. It's difficult to count the number of occasions I fell asleep in class after spending most of my morning in traffic. There were moments when I arrived near the end of a lecture, and as a result, decided to skip class. I did not see the value in receiving only a portion of the lesson, so grabbing something to eat while waiting for my next class seemed like a better use of my energy.

When I missed class, I should have made an appointment with the teach-ing assistant or professor to make-up the material. This additional effort could have helped the teaching assistant and professor to explain the content of the course better. It could have helped them to get to know me beyond another student with a university identification number on their roster. However, as a young man groomed in an education system and culture that emphasized individualism, I believed that going to ask for help was a sign of weakness.

As one of few Black male students in predominately White courses, I felt the pressure of representing the entire Black race. Every time I raised my hand in class or had a conversation with my professor, I thought every word was perceived as a representation of every Black student on campus. Attending office hours may have demonstrated to the professor or teaching assistant that I was a student who was serious about understanding the mate-rial and the final grade, but I found it incredibly difficult to get rid of the negative belief system that plagued my previous school experiences. There was a plethora of other positive possibilities in attending office hours, but I was unable to comprehend them as a Black male student groomed in the US educational system.

In the semester I took Math 090, all students were assigned homework every week and it was not collected or calculated as part of the final grade. Homework offered an additional opportunity to practice the concepts taught in class and prepare for the exams, but I did not have the discipline or the desire to complete the assignments while knowing that no one would evaluate the work. My previous schooling experiences told me math was not my stron-gest subject, and so I didn't put much effort into class, homework, and exams. The assumptions that I had about my performance in math were similar to other Black males and remains a well-documented phenomenon (Cheema & Galluzzo, 2013, Kannapel et al., 2005; Scafidi & Bui, 2010).

I was convinced I did not enjoy math and that belief was the steering wheel that drove my work ethic. I frequently did well in classes that required writing, reading and critical thinking skills. However, in math I often struggled to earn passing grades and couldn't find the motivation to work with the same intensity applied in other subjects. At this point, I had not adopted the mentality that consistency and discipline could have a positive impact on my ability to learn and grow in multiple capacities including math.

I did not have an accountability group or the self-discipline to complete homework for Math 090 without the threat of tangible consequences. While I had friends in my classes, we did not get together out of class to ensure that we consistently studied or completed homework. Occasionally we would meet to review for an exam, but these sessions were frequently interrupted with conversations not relative to the subject. The combination of a lack of discipline, accountability, and being underprepared for college-level math resulted in a failing grade during my first semester at UIC.

I was extremely disappointed in myself for failing my first college course. The setback reinforced the limited beliefs I had of myself to succeed in college. It reminded me of my high school's counselors lack of faith in my ability to succeed at a university immediately following graduation. I also understood this failure as confirmation that there was nothing I could do to improve in math. The failure of Math 090 brought many underlying emotions and internal battles with self-doubt to the surface. It wasn't until later in life that I was able to see how failure could lead to future positive outcomes.

I needed to make better choices in scheduling, developing more discipline toward my academics, and challenge notions of Black masculinity to be successful in college. With regards to my class schedule, I decided never to enroll in a class at 8 am unless I was willing to leave my home at 5 am to avoid traffic. I learned I needed to do the homework, regardless of how pointless it seemed, because it provided me with additional practice time outside of class. It was time to challenge antiquated social constructs that equated asking for help with weakness. As I identified paths that would lead to success in college, I began to change my approach.

I entered college as a Liberal Arts and Sciences' student with an undeclared major as part of the alternative admissions option. There were several majors that I was interested in, but none stood out among the rest. The College of Business still appealed to me, but after the academic struggles, I experienced with algebra it was not a likely transfer option. I began to think I would enjoy a career in education, law, or politics, so in my sophomore year, I took courses that were more in alignment with these fields.

As a Political Science student, I took a course called the *Social and Political Foundations of Philosophy*. The course explored the writings of European philosophers such as Jean-Jacques Rousseau, David Hume, and John Locke. I was required to read chapters from an edited textbook, write two 4–7 page papers, and actively participate in class discussions. Of the course's requirements, I believed I would excel in the reading and writing requirements.

The classes were marginally interesting; I had a difficult time with the assignments and finding the courage to express my opinion during lectures. My writing lacked clarity and did not illustrate that I understood the material covered in class. After years of being convinced that students who do not speak in class earn better grades because they do not interrupt the teacher's lesson plans, it was difficult to meet the expectations of engaging dialogue with my college professors.

The schools I attended before college emphasized sitting down and being quiet. My teachers' "sit down and shut-up" approach to classroom management that is frequently the protocol in schools of color was difficult to distance myself from in college. In high school, things started to change for me in my classes when I decided to remain in my seat and not talk to anyone. I stopped receiving detentions for behavior categorized as disruptive and disrespectful. I learned students were rewarded when they sat quietly and only spoke when the teacher asked for their opinion.

In college, the expectation was that students come prepared to engage the material by vocalizing their observations and asking questions during lectures. Many professors called on students who raised their hands but expected everyone to interject a comment or question during class. Occasionally I would find the courage to let myself become vulnerable and speak in class, but that was few and far in between my comfortable decisions to remain quiet. While I found the topics in the philosophy course of my second-year thought-provoking, I found it difficult to initiate discussions with other students, the teaching assistant, and especially the professor.

My philosophy professor had a heavy English accent and talked like the dead men we studied in class. When he lectured, it was difficult to escape the feeling that I was hearing Jean-Jacques Rousseau's or David Hume's reincarnated voices. I felt intimidated by my professor's command of the subject, and I did not identify with the content of the course. It was obvious he was passionate about the topics and that being a professor of philosophy was central to his identity.

On the first day of class, my philosophy professor passed out the syllabus and explained the assignments to seventy-four other students and me. He said we would not be tested via a multiple choice exam on the reading assignments, but instead on our ability to read, comprehend, analyze, and write about the philosophers' perspectives. These assignments were central to the course, along with active participation in the lectures and discussion sections led by his teaching assistant. The professor highlighted the assignments' due dates and emphasized the importance of coming prepared for each class with questions and comments about the readings.

When I received the syllabus, I took a mental note of when the assignments were due and placed it in my folder. Throughout the semester I would take the syllabus out to verify the reading schedule, but I failed to pay attention to the due dates for the writing assignments. In the seventh week of classes, the professor reminded us our midterm papers were due on Friday. While I was aware of the topics and readings assigned each week, I did not complete each assignment or begin the process of writing the paper.

Due to my lack of preparation in class lectures, I was unclear on many of the philosophers' stances, which was critical to the essay that required a comprehensive understanding of the material. During class, I had questions that would have assisted in providing me with clarity, but I was convinced that being quiet in class was the best way to absorb the material, earn good grades, and gain recognition as a good student. It is possible that my questions or comments would have enabled my peers and me to gain insight into the topics. This improved understanding of the subject may have encouraged me to begin the paper earlier than the night before the paper was due. There was a host of potential outcomes that went unrealized due to the inadequate preparation I received for success as a Black male in K-12 schools.

I frequently attended classes that lacked the critical pedagogy necessary for Black boys to do well in school and make connections between the curriculum and their lives. In college, I was unaware of the research indicating that academic underachievement often is related to the failure of schools to implement critical pedagogy and employ teachers of color with whom Black males can feel connected (Foster, 1995; Giroux, 2001; Kincheloe, 2005; Lynn, 1999). However, my experiences with irrelevant courses and limited experiences with Black male teachers convinced me of its reality. I did not have the same tools as other college students, but I tried to follow the study habits I believed made them successful.

I pulled an all-nighter working on the midterm writing assignment for my philosophy course to ensure that I turned it in on time. Despite the lack of sleep the previous night, I somehow arrived at campus without getting into a car accident, and I was happy I managed to complete the assignment by the due date. Full of caffeine and optimism that I had cracked the code to college success, I turned in my paper to the teaching assistant. I let out a sigh of relief after the teaching assistant collected the papers and told the class to expect everything returned in about two weeks.

The following two weeks appeared to drag as I waited in anticipation for my paper to be returned. With the confidence gained from surviving my first all-nighter, I became convinced I put in enough effort to receive an "A" on the writing assignment. I knew I was not clear in some of the analysis components of the paper, but I believed that meeting the page requirements was the most critical part of earning the grade I desired. The day our papers were scheduled to be returned, I arrived at class early because I was eager to see my grade on the longest paper I had written up to that date. In anticipation of receiving positive feedback and the "A" I believed I had earned, I smiled and sat upright in my seat. When the teaching assistant returned my paper, the smile that I had entered the room with quickly left along with my optimism.

The teaching assistant decided that I earned a "D" on the midterm writing assignment. I internalized this "D" as another indicator I wasn't fit for college. It was challenging for me to understand how failing this assignment was an opportunity for me to attend office hours, visit the writing center, and ultimately learn how to improve for the next paper I would be assigned to write. I knew college was different from high school and understood that anything less than a "C" was essentially a failing grade.

I was upset because I believed my writing skills were strong. Math was not a strong academic area, but reading and writing I thought were among my strengths as a student. The paper I submitted was full of grammatical and typographical errors that were the result of my procrastination. These avoidable mistakes, in combination with the lack of clarity on many of the philosophers' ideas, prevented me from earning the grade I desired.

When I failed the math course in my freshman year, my sister Erica asked me if I ever attended office hours or talked to the professor. When I replied no to taking the time to participate in office hours, she scolded me. I remember the conversation like it was yesterday.

She said, "Yellow Monkey, that is the problem. You must go and talk with the professor or teaching assistant because they can give you more attention in a one-on-one setting. I learned this after struggling in some of my courses during freshman year. It is imperative to make time and meet with the professor or teaching assistant to improve your chances of doing well in college."

Remembering this conversation with my sister, I sent the philosophy professor an email for an appointment to discuss my progress and develop a plan to improve my grade by the end of the semester. He agreed to meet with me during his office hours of the following week. Although I was a student in his class, I had never spoken to him, and I wasn't sure he knew my name among the other seventy-four students in his freshman course. I was nervous to meet with him, but I knew it was necessary to prevent failing the semester.

A week later, I arrived on time for my appointment and knocked at my professor's office door for permission to enter. "Yes, come in," he called.

"Hello, my name is Vernon Lindsay, and I am a student in your Philosophy 101 course. I emailed you about a meeting to discuss my midterm paper and to create a plan that can help me improve my grade."

"Yes, I recall the email. Please have a seat and let's take a look at your paper."

I pulled my paper out of my two-pocket folder and handed it to my professor. It seemed like the ten minutes he took to read my paper and scan the teaching assistant's comments went on for hours. Finally, he looked up and began to form a response.

"You're a good writer. Some sentence structure errors could have been avoided with proofreading, but otherwise, I can follow your arguments. Your understanding of the material is not in alignment with the perspectives I present in class, but I can understand your logic. Have you ever visited the Writing Center?"

After an awkward pause, I responded. "No."

I didn't admit it, but I did not know a Writing Center existed! The professor said, "You have to take advantage of the resources that are available to you as a student at UIC. The Writing Center is a good campus resource that can help you to create clear sentences that will better enable your reader to make more sense of the ideas presented in your paper. The additional set of eyes will help prevent some of the simple errors made in your writing." Then, he turned to look at his computer and pulled up the website for the campus' writing center. He showed me their hours, locations, and the types of services they provided.

I was not taking advantage of all the resources available to me on campus. The Writing Center appeared to offer the exact services I needed to improve my grades on future assignments. My professor recommended that I visit the Writing Center in advance of the final paper's due date, to prevent losing points for minor errors. I agreed to make it a priority for the final and in the future with other assignments. I walked away from that meeting with the belief my professors and the academic centers on campus were valuable resources that could help me to do my best. Riding the emotional high that came after a positive meeting with my professor, I was determined to do better in philosophy for about a week before I began to return to my familiar ways.

There were some days that were better than others, but there was something lacking from the course. I was interested in some of the conversations that took place during the discussion sections, but most of the time I found the class boring. Reading the books and articles for class felt too abstract and not applicable to my life. I had this unshakeable feeling that there was something missing from the philosophical ideas that were presented in class and it prevented me from bringing my best effort.

Somehow, I made it through to the end of the semester and earned a "C" in the course. Starting the final paper early and visiting the Writing Center were invaluable strategies that led to a better grade on the final writing assignment. I decided that starting the writing process early would be a method I would use in the future to improve my performance on similar assignments. It was obvious this approach impacted my final grade, and I was optimistic that it would produce similar outcomes the following semester.

As I was in the process of selecting my courses for the semester after the philosophy course, I talked with one of my friends about my experiences. I told my friend, Whitney, I was happy to be done with philosophy because I found the books and articles outdated. It was really difficult for me to understand the authors' arguments and it showed in my papers. Whitney listened to me and then recommended that I check out a course in the African-American Studies department.

I never thought about taking a course in African-American studies before Whitney mentioned the idea. Frequently, I participated in open-mic poetry events where many of the poets talked about Black history and current events, but I didn't see college as the place to explore these topics further. I was unaware that positive self-awareness had the potential to lead to success in any future endeavor. Whitney took a course called *African-American Religious Traditions* during the semester I struggled with philosophy, and he said it was the best course he had ever taken at UIC. He said that because I was into poetry and "Black stuff," the course would fit in alignment with my interests.

In my second year of college, I began to develop a strong interest in Black studies. My interest in the subject was not due to any class I had ever taken in school. I was drawn to this history because of my involvement in Chicago's open mic poetry scene. Nearly every Tuesday evening I attended a poetry set at a café not far from campus called Java Oasis.

At the Java Oasis, I frequently heard poems about the historical contributions by people of African descent who were relatively unknown to me. Poets and spoken word artists often talked about the knowledge of self, and being well versed in Black history was central to this concept. When I began to attend poetry sets, I possessed a cursory understanding of Black history and frequently shared my poems that described my relationships with women. However, the more I listened to other poets the desire to explore Black history was cultivated.

I was familiar with Civil Rights era icons such as Dr. Martin Luther King Jr. and Rosa Parks, from my K-12 school experiences. However, beyond their significant contributions and a topical understanding of slavery, I was uneducated about the history of people of African descent. Chicago poets wore t-shirts that reflected their words about Imhotep, George Jackson, Huey P. Newton, Kwame Nkrumah, Assata Shakur, Nikki Giovani and other significant figures in the older and more modern lives of African people. When I went to open mic events where poets recited pieces reflective of deep exploration through self-discovery in history, I listened in awe wishing I knew more about my ancestors.

When my friend, Whitney, mentioned the *African-American Religious Traditions* course after I talked about the challenges I faced in other classes, I saw it as an opportunity. It was an opportunity to earn college credit and learn more about a side of history that was not part of my earlier experiences in school. Whitney's course recommendation also appealed to me because I was raised in a Black church pastored by my father. I was interested in how the material would align with or refute what I had come to accept as my faith.

The class was taught by Professor Conewest, who worked in the African-American Studies department as an Adjunct Professor. He was a tall Black man who wore glasses and his hair styled in long dreadlocks that went beyond his shoulders. From the first day of class, I knew that Conewest had a deep connection to the material. He had this gift to speak with authority and confidence that demanded respect. Professor Conewest was my first Black professor in college, and he helped me discover what was possible when you align your passion with a vision for your life.

The reading and writing assignments assigned in Conewest's class were challenging, but I had an interest in the subject that went beyond a grade in the course. We read literature by Cornel West, Patricia Hill Collins, Gayraud Wilmore, Kelly Brown Douglas, John Blassingame, James Cone, and a host of other historians and theologians to understand religion, spirituality, and sexuality from an African perspective. As students in Professor Conewest's course, we were required to write weekly reflection papers where we summarized the assigned readings, critiqued the author's perspective, and analyzed how we related to the material. The reading assignments and weekly reflection writing assignments took my level of comprehension to a level unmatched in my previous philosophy and math courses.

In many of my other subjects, I associated homework with chores I wanted to avoid. *African American Religious Traditions* was different, because of my genuine interest in the topic and Professor Conewest's dynamic approach to every class session. Conewest had a unique way of explaining the material and stimulating great discussions among students. The combination of the subject matter and class culture inspired me to do my best in school unlike any other time in my life.

My effort and ability to prioritize my responsibilities during the semester I was enrolled in *African-American Religious Traditions* paid off; I earned an "A" in the course, but, more importantly, I became interested in African-American Studies as a major. The rigor of the course, alongside learning from a Black male professor, inspired me to make the most of my time at UIC. It also fostered a belief that I could also follow in the footsteps of Conewest and become a professor.

Because of my positive experiences as a student in Professor Conewest's class, I decided to change my major from Political Science to African-American Studies. It was clear to me that in making that decision I would develop a deeper understanding and appreciation of Black history. In becoming an African-American Studies' major, I believed I would get to know more about myself from professors of color, who had a genuine interest in seeing me succeed. I was stoked by the idea of learning more about my history from people of color who I believed understood more about my experiences as a Black male striving toward an education in America.

As a student of African-American studies, I found the courage to share my opinions in class and to seek assistance when I experienced setbacks. In addition to taking courses with Professor Conewest, I had the honor of also being a student of other prominent and upcoming Black scholars. Their course content and instructional quality enabled me to graduate with academic distinction in four years with a major in African-American Studies and a minor in Political Science.

From the initial rejection letter to UIC's College of Business to graduating in four years as one of the few Black males in my class, I learned a lot about myself. One of the key takeaways included the understanding that failure could not define my potential. This lesson of realizing potential through failure came from my challenges to pass freshman algebra and inability to connect with the material in philosophy. It was the power of community and my ability to see myself in the curriculum that also led to the success I created with others as an African-American Studies' student. I had some challenges in undergrad that, unbeknownst to me at the time, would prepare me for that hostile environment commonly referred to as graduate school.

What does this narrative indicate about Black males and the opportunities available in college?

There is often a debate about whether we should prepare all Black males to attend college. Too frequently college campuses ignore the implications of race on the K-12 school experiences of students of color, and expect all students to arrive with equitable abilities and study skills. The experiences I discussed in my undergraduate narrative, other critical issues facing Black males on campuses, along with the financial investment to attend college make attendance a valid concern. All Black males do not have parents that can provide the emotional or financial support to assist with college, and as the research of Shaun Harper (2012) confirms, a strong family unit is essential to increase undergraduate degree achievements among Black males. While I believe it is not critical to attend college to achieve success in life, college can offer Black males resources and options that are not as easily accessible off-campus.

When I graduated from undergrad, I earned a departmental award in African American-Studies, which came with a monetary gift to help cover my expenses to travel to Ethiopia. As an African-American Studies major, I resonated with the philosophical and practical ideas of building a Pan-African community. In my senior year, there was an opportunity to assist a community literacy initiative in Ethiopia. I talked with my professors about my desire to participate, and they nominated me for the award that empowered me to acquire the necessary resources for the trip and to contribute toward a remarkable initiative.

College does not always lead to employment or financial success for Black males, but it can foster a positive environment to learn more about yourself. Since visiting Ethiopia for the first time, I returned on two separate occasions and traveled to places such as Brazil, Benin, Cameroon, and Mexico. Each of these trips was inspired by seeds planted in me during college to experience diverse cultures and explore the histories of people who are often undervalued in society. Too often Black males are faced with limited economic choices after high school which can lead to poor decisions. College can enable the possibility of Black males to learn more about themselves which is critical in the journey to create personal and professional success.

Through my experiences in college, I was able to understand that failure is a part of the human existence and it can create learning opportunities that are necessary for growth and improvement. For Black males including myself, the challenge is to accept that we all fail, but can use our failures as encouragement to accomplish things others deem impossible. The lack of preparation I experienced in undergrad was just a fraction of the challenges that I would experience in graduate school.

To download the FREE PDF workbook and instructional guide, please visit: www.vlindsayphd.com/crtblackmales

References

Cheema, J. R., & Galluzzo, G. (2013). Analyzing the gender gap in math achievement: Evidence from a large-scale US sample. *Research in Education*, 90(1), 98–112.

Fischer, R. (2004). Standardization to account for cross-cultural response bias: A classification of score adjustment procedures and review of research in JCCP. *Journal of Cross-Cultural Psychology*, 35(3), 263–282.

Foster, M. (1995). African American teachers and culturally relevant pedagogy. In J. A. Banks & C. A. M. Banks (Eds.), *Handbook of research on multicultural education* (pp. 570–581). New York, NY: Macmillan.

Giroux, H. A. (2001). *Theory and resistance in education: Towards a pedagogy for the opposition* (Rev. ed.). Westport, CT: Bergin & Garvey.

Harper, S. R. (2012). *Black male student success in higher education: A report from the National Black Male College Achievement Study*. University of Pennsylvania, Graduate School of Education, Center for the Study of Race and Equity in Education.

Helms, J. E. (1992). Why is there no study of cultural equivalence in standardized cognitive ability testing? *American Psychologist, 47*(9), 1083 -1101.

Horsford, S. D., & Grosland, T. (2013). Badges of inferiority: The racialization of achievement in US education. In M. Lynn & A. D. Dixson (Eds.), *Handbook of critical race theory in education* (pp. 153–166). New York, NY: Routledge.

Kannapel, P. J., Clements, S. K., Taylor, D., & Hibpshman, T. (2005). Inside the black box of high-performing high-poverty schools. *Report, Prichard Committee for Academic Excellence.*

Kincheloe, J. (2005). *Critical pedagogy.* New York, NY: Peter Lang.

Lynn, M. (1999). Toward a critical race pedagogy: A research note. *Urban Education, 33*(5), 606–626.

Scafidi, T., & Bui, K. (2010). Gender similarities in math performance from middle school through high school. *Journal of Instructional Psychology, 37*(3), 252–256.

Solórzano, G. D., & Yosso, J. T. (2016). Critical race methodology: Counter-storytelling as an analytical framework for educational research. In E. Taylor, D. Gillborn, & G. Ladson-Billings (Eds.), *Foundations of critical race theory in education* (pp. 127–153). New York, NY: Routledge.

· 6 ·

FROM PRETTY BOY TO MAN

Introduction

Near the end of the graduate program that I was enrolled in at the University of Illinois at Chicago, I called my father on the verge of tears. As a grown man, I still could not get myself to cry in his presence or over the phone because of the seeds of Black masculinity planted in me as a boy who others called pretty. I called my father on the phone because I was going through a really difficult period in graduate school that forced me into thoughts of quitting; I wanted to be vulnerable, but my masculinity roots were so strong I could not allow a tear to fall from my eye.

I was accused of stealing research from a professor who I had worked with for four years. It was an extremely difficult accusation to accept because I believed our relationship had grown beyond teacher and student. We were friends and professional colleagues. At the time, I was angry, upset, and full of rage. I revisited feelings of hostility toward education and my teachers that were central to my belief system that began in the third grade. The ordeal in graduate school kept me up at night and forced me back into a state of depression that I experienced after high school when I didn't believe I would get admitted to college.

When I was a PhD student in the University of Illinois at Chicago's College of Education, I experienced a significant number of challenges. On many evenings, I attended classes where I was one of few males of color enrolled. I often felt I did not belong in graduate school and on one occasion withdrew from a course to prevent a failing grade from appearing on my transcript. After many years of working with an esteemed professor, my status as a PhD candidate was threatened due to some of my careless mistakes and poor communication. While graduate school was difficult, today I am grateful for everything that happened because it taught me perseverance in the face of intense opposition.

There are many obstacles Black males will encounter en route to and after admittance to graduate programs that are influenced by the intersections of race, racism, and masculinity. It was my experience and that of other Black males whom I have encountered throughout the United States that daily self-doubt and isolation in advanced degree educational settings are often part of the process. Feelings of not being "good enough" as a student of color, coupled with isolation from family and friends, can influence the decision to continue or prematurely exit a graduate program (Ellis, 2001; Hall & Burns, 2009; Scott, 2017). These feelings of racial inferiority that can surface in graduate school can be especially difficult for Black males who via dominant masculinity constructs are unaware of positive ways to channel anger, frustration, and loneliness. Without a deep level of commitment, the belief in an unknown future, and support from a community it can be difficult and in some cases impossible for many Black males to finish graduate school.

I was on the verge of quitting several times as revealed in the narrative for this chapter. The process to earn a doctoral degree was by far the most difficult leg of my educational journey. In the story that proceeds, I aim to avoid defaming the character of anyone involved; pseudonyms were used, and other measures were taken to protect the identity of all related parties. I acknowledge my mistakes in graduate school and in retrospect understand the perspective of the highly respectable professor who was merely doing his best to maintain the integrity of the research. Today, I can understand and appreciate what I experienced in graduate school, but at the time I did not know how I could continue.

Throughout this narrative, I try my best to present both sides of the ordeal for you as the reader to decipher the truth. I share my experiences in graduate school so that others will understand how important perseverance is in the process to achieve advanced degrees. My experiences taught me that as a

Black male, you must possess a spirit of relentless dedication to earn a graduate or professional degree. There were many challenges that I endured in graduate school, but I wouldn't change any component of my story. Each obstacle eventually led to the person I am today.

From Pretty Boy to Man

I attended orientation for graduate school in the College of Education at UIC on a Wednesday evening in the Fall semester of 2007. As I sat in the commons room with approximately thirty other people, some faculty, and other students, I realized the moment had finally arrived for me to pursue a doctoral degree. I was excited and anxious to start, because like others (McCallum, 2017), I believed earning a PhD would allow me to make a substantial impact in my community. My former professors in the African-American studies department inspired me to pursue a doctoral degree, and it was finally time to show them and others I could achieve the unthinkable as a student of the Policy Studies in Urban Education program.

Before orientation, I was in contact with a professor and an advanced graduate student who I will call Marcus, with regards to an opportunity to join a research team. We talked about a new research assistant position that offered valuable field experience, a monthly stipend, and a tuition waiver. It was also an excellent opportunity to mentor a group of Black males and to contribute to a valuable study that explored recent policy changes in a nearby high school. I was excited about the research position because it offered me field experiences, the opportunity to mentor youth, and financial assistance to pay for graduate school.

As I sat in orientation and listened to the information about the program, I also combed the room to look for Marcus. We talked on the phone and through email the previous night and agreed to meet in-person at the orientation for the first time. Based on our conversation, I knew he was a Black male, so I scanned the room looking for other students who looked like me. The College of Education reflected the impact of systemic racism within the United States' education system where students of color are often not provided with adequate resources to prepare them to attend graduate school. There were only three Black males in the room including a faculty member and myself. Through process of elimination, I assumed the other person who I did not know was Marcus.

My assumptions were correct, and he walked up to me after the orientation to introduce himself. We sat and talked for about fifteen minutes about our backgrounds and the research project he was actively involved in as a graduate assistant. He was from Los Angeles and moved to Chicago to attend graduate school. As a second-year student, he shared with me some advice on the classes I should take and the ones to avoid. He talked about being one of the few Black males in the program, his feelings of isolation, and how important it was for us to remain connected with each other for support. In his responsibilities as a graduate assistant, he offered me some insights into the scope of the research study I desperately wanted to join.

The research site was located at a high school where students were required to meet specific requirements before they were admitted. Grades, attendance, and socioeconomic status were among the criteria. As a research assistant, I was told my responsibilities for the study would include mentoring a group of Black males and gathering data about a university co-sponsored initiative. The position sounded ideal to me, but before I could allow myself to get too excited, I needed to meet with the lead investigator, Dr. H, who was a professor at the university.

To say I was nervous before meeting Dr. H is an understatement; I was terrified and also thrilled because he was a highly regarded and notable professor with the power to determine my fate for the position. Despite my trepidations, I found him kind and relatable. We talked for over an hour discussing the project and how I believed I could contribute. I told him about some of my experiences in education and my reasons for wanting to join the study. At the end of the meeting, I was convinced I would gain valuable research experience as an assistant and make a positive impact on the lives of younger Black males.

Before I left Dr. H's office, I thought I would be offered the position as a research assistant. I didn't understand how things worked in graduate school. After the professor identifies a potential research assistant, they are required to get approval from an administrator. The budget is verified, an applicant's eligibility is reviewed, and another administrator sends out the necessary paperwork. It's not a simple process.

About five days after our meeting, I received a phone call from Dr. H informing me of his decision. I was approved to join the study and needed to complete some paperwork before it could be made official. Excited, relieved, and nervous are just a few of the emotions I felt after my call ended with Dr. H. A few days later, a representative from the university's human resources department emailed me the necessary documents that explained the position, the tuition waiver, and monthly stipend. I eagerly accepted all conditions, responded to the email from human resources, and joined the research team.

For four years, I worked as a research assistant collecting data and forming relationships with students, administrators, teachers, and faculty from a nearby high school. The university funded three of the four years to ensure the study's objectives were met. Marcus moved on to a different position, as did other graduate students who joined the project at various points to assist in the collection process. During this time, I gathered a significant amount of data to fulfill the objectives of multiple studies.

A part of the work I did as a graduate research assistant was the facilitation of an extracurricular program designed to build relationships with the students and provide academic support. In alignment with critical race theory, the research took a direct approach to analyzing and addressing inequalities derived from the intersections between race and racism (Stovall, 2013). I worked with a representative of the high school, Dr. H, Marcus and other graduate students to develop robust services for a group of young Black males. The action-oriented research included workshops in the African Brazilian martial of Capoeira, community service projects, overnight camping experiences, after-school tutoring, and a host of other activities that were designed to form relationships, strengthen academic skills, and build community.

Throughout the gathering of data for the focal research project, I had multiple conversations with Dr. H about permission to use a portion of the findings to complete my dissertation. It was agreed upon that when I reached the final stage of the PhD program, I would have complete access and use of data from the more extensive study to include in my findings. Despite changes in the structure of the research project, there was no indication to believe the conditions of our arrangement had changed throughout my time in the Policy Studies in Urban Education program.

While I worked on the research project, I was also enrolled in full-time courses that were in alignment with my concentration in the social foundations of education. I took classes that explored issues in education and analyzed the persistence of race, racism, gender, and other social constructions. I was often one of only a few Black males in my classes, and much like the experiences Marcus shared with me at orientation, I had a difficult time forming a community. Throughout, multiple courses I didn't feel I belonged in graduate school and wanted to quit. While there were other students enrolled in the program, I was one of few Black men and often lacked the support from my peers to hold me accountable for success.

During one of my semesters in grad school, I enrolled in a course that explored quantitative methodology. It focused on the use of statistics to make sense of research data in education and it was consistent with other doctoral programs where administrators create degree requirements that influence student outcomes (McAlpine & Norton, 2006). As a research assistant, I believed the course could add value to my work and it was mandatory to satisfy a requirement of the doctoral program. My K-12 experiences in math and beliefs that I could not excel in the subject resurfaced on the first day of class and haunted me throughout the semester. Limited thinking and the lack of community put me in a position at the end of the quantitative methodology where I needed to request an incomplete grade or receive an "F" on my transcript.

I struggled throughout the semester with the quantitative methods course. Early poor educational experiences in math convinced me that it was not my strong suit, so I came to class ill-prepared to succeed. I returned to my former methods from Math 090 in not completing the homework that would have better prepared me for the exams. After two semesters, I managed to pass the course because I took time to meet with the professor, attended the teaching assistant's office hours, and established determination within me to master the subject. There were more than a couple of moments when I wanted to quit, but I kept pushing toward the goal of earning a doctoral degree to make an impact in my community.

After four years of challenging coursework and research experiences, I was elated to make it to the stage where I could conduct independent research. The dissertation proposal I submitted to my committee reflected the knowledge, talents, and skills acquired throughout grad school. In the four years leading up to writing the proposal, I was guided by two professors, my Advisor, and Dr. H, who ensured I understood the process to produce quality research.

When the time came for me to defend my proposal orally, Dr. H communicated with a group of professors to determine the time and location for me to present my planned study. I began the defense with an introduction that explained my connection to the material. I talked about my experiences as a Black male in high school and the suspension I served for not wearing my identification card. My personal stories from K-12 institutions were shared to demonstrate a connection to my research subjects who were a group of young Black males and to reflect the value of my experiential knowledge consistent with critical race theory methodological framework (Solórzano & Yosso,

2002). The proposal defense established the importance of the study to provide a platform for the voices of young Black men to be heard in hopes that they may be able to influence school policy and school culture.

Following the introduction, I discussed the relevant research to the experiences of Black males who attend K-12 schools. I talked about Black males' experiences with race and racism in educational settings as documented by notable researchers in the field. Then I proceeded with details of how the research I proposed to use for my dissertation was an extension of a larger project and how it would make a significant contribution to the field. It took a lot of preparation for my proposal's defense, but through the four years of challenging classes and research experiences, I was confident in the outcome.

After my presentation, I answered a series of questions aimed to expand my methodologies and identify measures to improve my preliminary data. Due to my experiences in the field and working on a portion of the data for four years, I had a plan in motion to collect the remaining data. The professors who were part of my committee helped me to expand my plan and consider additional resources to investigate how resistance behaviors among Black males could be used to transform school cultures. Each professor, including Dr. H, who was among the top intellectuals of their field, approved my oral research proposal; I took one more step toward a doctoral degree.

Because I collected a surplus of data while working as a research assistant, I was advanced in the process to complete my dissertation. Before the proposal and confirmed during my oral exam, I established with Dr. H an arrangement to use data from the more extensive study in my doctoral thesis. I needed to complete some additional interviews with the students during their senior year, but anything collected throughout my term as a research assistant we agreed I could use as part of my study.

This understanding of data usage was clear to every member of my committee who acted as mentors to me throughout the dissertation phase. There were some additional interviews to collect, but otherwise, I had gathered a significant amount of field observations, interviews, and other data applicable to my topic. With this head start, it enabled me to schedule the recommended interviews with the students and begin the writing process.

I worked every day on my dissertation for four months between February and June of 2012. With the discipline I practiced, in addition to some preliminary articles I worked on throughout the four years of the larger study, I was prepared for a quick turnaround to defend my research. My timeline was atypical because many students take a minimum of one year to complete a dissertation following an oral research proposal defense. However, due to prior writing projects that included a book with Dr. H, I believed I was ready to defend my dissertation and graduate within six months after presenting my proposal.

My Advisor and I were in contact with each other throughout the four months it took me to collect the remaining data and to write my dissertation. He reviewed drafts of each chapter and offered me feedback to improve the grammar and content. I revised several versions of my dissertation until it reached a point my Advisor and I believed it was ready to orally defend in front of the other members of my committee. We scheduled a date, and I meticulously took time to prepare myself for the defense. The day before I was scheduled to defend my dissertation I received a phone call from Dr. H that would break my spirit and turn my enthusiasm into anger.

I had just finished grocery shopping when my cell phone rang. "Hello?" "Hello Vernon, how are you?"

"Dr. H hey, how's it going? How was your trip?" Because we frequently talked, I knew he had just returned from an academic conference out of the country.

"It went well, thank you for asking. Listen, I'm calling you because I had some time on the plane to really comb through your dissertation and we have a problem."

"A problem, what's the issue?"

"Well I know that you are scheduled to defend your dissertation tomorrow, but I will not go through with it. I read your dissertation, and I believe there is data that was stolen from my office."

"Excuse me, what do you mean stolen?"

"I read your dissertation, and there is data included that I do not have in my possession. I believe you conducted an alternative study at our research site, without my knowledge."

"What? That is the furthest thing from the truth. I used the data that you authorized me to collect. We are working on a book contract together, and I would have no advantage in keeping data from you."

The conversation continued for another fifteen minutes and when the call ended it was clear I would not have an opportunity to defend my dissertation as initially scheduled. I was deeply disturbed by the accusation I stole data from my research supervisor. In reaching the highest level of education, I was forced to remember how the intersections of race, racism, and gender haunt the Black male experience. I had to confront the dominant images of Black males as prone to criminal activity that others often impose on us (Harper & Davis, 2012). When I received that phone call, I was firmly reminded that at any level of education, negative assumptions of what it means to be Black and male can persist.

I've never viewed school as a tool to escape or deny my identity as a Black male. When I switched my major to African-American studies in undergrad, school became a resource to further channel the positive self-awareness critical to success in life. It was never my intention or desire to remove myself from connecting with other Black men and boys through the opportunities earning a PhD can provide. A big part of the reason I began to pursue a doctoral degree was because I aimed to make a larger impact on the lives of young Black males. In the process of earning a PhD, I did not expect to face charges of theft correlated with my identity as a young Black male.

As I hung up the phone after the conversation with Dr. H, I said to myself, "I can't believe this. The day before my defense. What am I going to do?"

I immediately called my Advisor and told him of the situation. He was shocked and could not believe the allegations. My Advisor said we have two options; we could proceed without Dr. H, which would come with another set of complications, or attempt to rectify the confusion through a series of meetings. I thought it would be best to arrange the meetings, where I could clarify my data sources, and directly address the concerns about the data.

Throughout the four years of the research study I was assigned to as a research assistant, the structure of the team and approach evolved. When I began the research project in my first semester of graduate school, I primarily worked alongside Marcus to meet the study's objectives as defined by Dr. H. Every Sunday, a digital copy of the collected field notes were emailed to Dr. H in preparation for our Monday meeting. At 10:00 am I met with Dr. H and Marcus every week to discuss the research objectives and to present hard copies of the previous week's field notes for storage in a locked filing cabinet.

This procedure of meeting on a weekly basis to discuss updates, turn in hard copies of the digital field notes, and to reevaluate methods was consistent for the first two years of the research study. In the third year of the study, Marcus accepted a high school teaching position and left the research project. Dr. H hired another graduate student who looked to me for leadership in the study's activities due to my seniority with the well-established methodology. As the senior research assistant, I took the lead on organizing research activities and facilitating many of the major components of the study.

In the third year of the research study, I increased my presence at the research site, and Dr. H became occupied with additional university-related responsibilities. Our schedules began to conflict, and we were unable to meet in person every week to discuss the study and turn in hard copies of the field notes. We remained in contact via email and phone, but our weekly in-person meetings eventually stopped.

The cancellation of our weekly meetings due to my additional work responsibilities at the research site and Dr. H's commitments at the university negatively impacted the research process. I should have insisted on keeping the meetings to preserve the process of sharing digital and hard copies of all the data gathered at the site. My decision to not maintain accurate records with Dr. H led to the belief that I purposely withheld data for personal gain.

Dr. H and I were contracted for a book project with a major academic publisher, and we also agreed to write a series of articles together with our findings. Due to these writing projects, I believed we would have ample time to sort, process, and analyze the data gathered on site. When our schedules became more full, the opportunities to meet came and went. Although we were planning to write a book together and other articles, we were not consistent with making time to plan and discuss the research after Marcus' transition to teaching high school.

When I received the phone call from Dr. H the day before I was scheduled to defend my dissertation, I thought it was ridiculous to think I would steal data. I had nothing to gain from withholding data, other than a dissertation that I knew he would review. Through conversations with other professors including my Advisor, I was able to get a better understanding of his perspective. The lapses in face-to-face meetings to discuss observations and interviews from the site convinced Dr. H I had conducted an alternative clandestine study. There was data in my dissertation he did not know existed.

I did not create an alternative investigation at the research site of the larger project I was assigned to as an assistant, but the lack of communication allowed for inconsistencies in the data available to all parties. For an entire year after I was initially scheduled to defend my dissertation, I had numerous meetings and countless email exchanges with Dr. H to clarify my usage of the data and proceed with my dissertation. These memos included an explanation of my actions and the steps I would take to correct my mistakes. I was required to revise, edit, and resubmit multiple versions of chapters from my dissertation to gain the rights to use a portion of the data I collected as part of the more extensive research study.

On multiple occasions, I complied with lengthy revision requests and soon after informed that I needed to make additional changes to protect the interests of Dr. H and the research subjects. It was tough and challenging. I called on every friend and family member who I could trust during this difficult time to listen to my concerns. Despite not having an emotionally vulnerable relationship with my father, I called him on multiple occasions for advice and his ear to my many complaints.

Throughout the process of writing my dissertation, I reached some high and low points in my life. My wife gave birth to our second child. With his birth, I became motivated to begin my mornings at 4:00 am where I sat at my desk to write. There were also evenings where I could not sleep because I was overtaken with anger, regret, and frustration.

On multiple days, when I received seemingly unsurmountable revision requests in addition to information that my character was being questioned among some of the faculty within the College of Education, I wanted to quit the program. I was tired of the strenuous email exchanges that described how I could use the findings. It felt impossible to satisfy every request and maintain the quality of the study I aimed to produce for my final thesis. There were times in my dissertation nightmare when I did not believe I would achieve my educational dream of earning a doctoral degree.

During this time, I frequently reflected in isolation and thought about other challenges I faced in school. In the third grade, I dealt with the feeling of being targeted by the Assistant Principal because I was a young Black boy. In middle school, I struggled with the performance of Black masculinity and the belief I was a thug who needed to fight to prove my self-worth. My experiences in high school revealed to me the lower expectations assigned to me due to my identity as a young Black male. In undergrad, I didn't believe in my ability to do well in math, and I allowed the constructs of masculinity to prevent me from getting help. Through these reflections, the affirmations from family and friends I realized that I had been through plenty in school as evidence I had the strength to not give up at this point.

I was motivated to finish the PhD in Policy Studies in Urban Education by the added responsibilities of that came with the blessings of fatherhood, a loving partner to an incredible woman, and a mentor to young Black males. The consistent reminder of who depended on me pushed me to write and respond with rational thought when I wanted to quit. As much as I wanted to leave the program, the impact I aimed to make in my community would not allow me to stop.

One year after the original date I was scheduled to defend my dissertation, I earned another opportunity to stand in front of my committee and present my research. I was well prepared for every potential objection to my findings and methodologies. Dr. H did not attend in person but called in over the phone. The hearing lasted one hour, and at the end, I was greeted for the first time as Dr. Lindsay.

What does this indicate about Black males and succeeding in graduate school?

In May of 2013, I stood on the stage at the University of Illinois at Chicago's pavilion with my right fist in the air as my name was called and a doctoral degree was conferred (Lindsay, 2015). I had plenty to be proud of in that moment of touching my educational dream. My ancestors paved a path for me, and with gratitude, I was able to navigate the road with an awareness of my identity as a Black male. The fist I put in the air at graduation was not only a nod to Tommie Smith and John Carlos who in the 1968 Olympics performed the Black Power salute as they received their medals but a testament to every-thing I experienced throughout the process from the third grade to earning a PhD in Policy Studies in Urban Education.

In the third grade, I began to feel that my identity as a young Black boy made me a target of my elementary school's administration. I didn't know how quite to articulate the impact racism made on my educational opportu-nities, but I felt a sense of hostility toward school and a disconnect between curricula and my life. Sure, I was not the best-behaved student in my classes, but there was more to my experience than the school was willing to see. An overwhelming number of images convinced me that self-defeating resistance behavior was central to my identity. As a Black boy, who my sisters and others called Yellow, I was confused.

In the fourth grade, I had my first tangible experience with someone who internalized racism and treated me as an inferior due to the color of my skin. Systemic and individual racism well informed Jennifer that Black people were inferior. Such internalized beliefs enabled her to reject my innocent romantic interests because in her words I was "colored." Coming from a racially isolated community on the Southside of Chicago, I didn't think much about how some people who identify as White might perceive me. This experience and others made me rethink my self-perception as a Black male born in America.

In middle school and high school, I continued to struggle with the indications of my identity as a Black male. I was convinced in a suburban environment, the performances of Black masculinity required me to embody a person full of rage. In middle school, I fought others to climb the ladder to acceptability camouflaged as popularity. In high school, I was suspended for not following the school's ID policy and told by a school counselor I did not have what it took to attend a university.

I experienced failure and other challenges in undergrad and graduate school, but I eventually earned a doctoral degree. With every stage of my education I have encountered obstacles, and through persistence, self-discipline, social consciousness, positive self-awareness, grace, and mercy I succeeded. I didn't do anything without the support of my parents, sisters, friends, teachers and other members of my community who believed in my potential. They saw something in me that I was unable to see in myself.

Black males must understand adopting an attitude of awareness and perseverance is critical to their success in education. Proponents of meritocracy will argue that Black males should only focus on working hard, and the successes they desire will be rewarded. Others will claim that for Black males to be successful, it simply involves having faith in the process and behaving like racism, sexism or other sociohistorical produced inequalities do not exist. I believe that as Black males we should always remain aware of injustices and use them as inspiration to build the internal perseverance necessary to achieve the impossible.

Black males must understand race and masculinity constructs exist and influence the way we view ourselves, communities, and academic potential. Racism is an American epidemic, which makes it imperative to discover ways to use education, initiate or assist movements of change. Some of us will need to engage protest or other acts of direct action, whereas others will need to be the person who creates awareness in our local jobs, entrepreneurial activities, and other circles of influence. Educators of Black males should help their students discover their unique contributions by continually seeking ways to make curricula relevant and through forming relationships that can help cultivate the positive self-awareness needed to take a stand against injustices.

If Black males are going to be successful in education, they will have to internalize their sources of inspiration, develop the discipline to cultivate positive self-awareness, and discover perseverance through challenges with the understanding that inequalities exist. This is not easy and will require resources such as empathetic mentors, caring teachers, and culturally relevant curricula. Throughout the dissertation ordeal, there was a part of me that wanted to quit, but I didn't because I believed my community needed me to complete the degree. I was a father to children who depended on me, a partner to a woman who supported me, and a mentor to young Black males who admired my unique talents, skills, and gifts. I was never convinced that somehow I could singlehandedly dismantle the school system. However, somewhere deep within me, there was a man who was called to make a substantial positive impact in my community and the lives of others.

To download the FREE PDF workbook and instructional guide, please visit: www.vlindsayphd.com/crtblackmales

References

Ellis, E. M. (2001). The impact of race and gender on graduate school socialization, satisfaction with doctoral study, and commitment to degree completion. *Western Journal of Black Studies, 25*(1), 30.

Hall, L., & Burns, L. (2009). Identity development and mentoring in doctoral education. *Harvard Educational Review, 79*(1), 49–70.

Harper, S. R., & Davis III, C. H. (2012). They (don't) care about education: A counternarrative on Black male students' responses to inequitable schooling. *The Journal of Educational Foundations, 26*(1/2), 103.

Lindsay, V. (2015) "The class that race built: Putting race at the center of a higher education course to challenge post-racialism in the United States and Brazil." *Journal of Higher Education Theory and Practice: 15,*(7), 11–24.

McAlpine, L., & Norton, J. (2006). Reframing our approach to doctoral programs: An integrative framework for action and research. *Higher Education Research & Development, 25*(1), 3–17.

McCallum, C. (2017). Giving back to the community: How African Americans envision utilizing their PhD. *The Journal of Negro Education, 86*(2), 138–153.

Scott, S. V. (2017). *The struggle is real: Black Doctoral Students' perceptions aspiring to the professoriate* (Doctoral dissertation). Temple University.

Solórzano, D. G., & Yosso, T. J. (2002). Critical race methodology: Counter-storytelling as an analytical framework for education research. *Qualitative Inquiry, 8*(1), 23–44.

Stovall, D. (2013). "Fightin' the Devil 24/7": Context, community and critical race praxis in education. In M. Lynn & A. D. Dixson (Eds.), *Handbook of critical race theory in education* (pp. 289–301). New York, NY: Routledge.

AFTERWORD

In the Fall semester of 2013, I returned to the University of Illinois at Chicago, because I accepted a position with the Honors College as a Postdoctoral Fellow in Teaching and Mentoring. In this role, I was responsible for teaching undergraduate courses, advising students in course selection, and co-directing a co-curricular program. I taught classes that explored the contemporary implications of racism in US schools, discussed career and entrepreneurial options after undergrad, and highlighted artistic movements among racialized people in Brazil.

Many of the stories shared in this text I also shared with my undergraduate students from the University of Illinois at Chicago's Honors College. The narratives served as opportunities to connect with my students about my experiences as a Black male in school and as tools to build bridges between the curriculum and their lives. In addition to my undergraduate students, the experiences I have shared in this book come from my experiences with teaching young people the African Brazilian martial art called Capoeira.

Capoeira was created by enslaved Africans in Brazil and combines elements of dance with acrobatics, music, self-defense, and rituals. I have studied Capoeira for 11 years and found it extremely useful to connect with young Black boys outside of the classroom. For seven years, I taught Capoeira in various capacities that included: a physical education teacher, research assistant, after-school facilitator, and an independent contractor.

I made use of Capoeira as a creative tool to engage Black males in a healthy mind and body activity. Each class involved physical movement and instruction in the percussion instruments that accompany the practice of this ancient art form born from resistance. I also took time in my classes to listen to the students' experiences in school and offer advice as necessary. Classes were provided to students in the city and south suburban schools of Chicago. My work with Capoeira allowed for multiple mentor/mentee relationships to be formed and served as an impetus for starting a business.

UCA Chicago L3c is the business I began in 2013 to offer young people and adults instruction in Capoeira and to extend consulting services to schools. Workshops took place at the elementary, high school, and college levels and shared the movements, music, history, and philosophies consistent with community, struggle, and resistance. I also worked with educators and administrators to create practical tools to engage youth in critical conversations about race and to discuss actions they could take to make an impact that extended beyond school walls. While my business was rewarding from a cultural and historical contribution perspective, it was not supplementing my income in a way that was sustainable long-term.

After three years of teaching undergraduate students at UIC and struggling to make ends meet through my business, I decided to do something bold. I declined a contract to renew my employment with UIC, sold many of my possessions and moved with my wife and three children to Mexico. It was not an easy decision, but it enabled me to dedicate myself to facilitating workshops, writing and seeking additional opportunities to share my stories and make an impact in schools.

Today, my business services include writing, consulting, and personal development coaching services. I write for several publications and work with individuals and organizations to create success strategies. With my wife and three children, I am a location-independent entrepreneur living in Mexico.

My family and I downsized our 3200 square foot home to ten suitcases and moved from our lives in Chicago, Illinois to Mazatlán, Sinaloa. On my family's YouTube channel, La Vida Lindsay, we share our challenges with learning Spanish and the adjustments that come along with moving abroad. With my family's move to Mexico, I have positioned myself to expand this work and its potential to inspire social changes around the world. The key now is to remember all the perseverance I gathered through my experiences in education, be patient, and understand everything that needs to happen will in due time.

Thank you for taking the time to read this work. For additional resources, please visit www.vlindsayphd.com and sign up for my mailing list.

BIBLIOGRAPHY

Altheide, D. L. (2009). The Columbine shootings and the discourse of fear. *American Behavioral Scientist, 52*(10), 1354–1370.

Bailey, P. (1983, August). A manchild of the 80s: Boys meet the challenge of growing up in Harlem. *USA Ebony*, pp. 68–72.

Brod, H., & Kaufman, M. (Eds.). (1994). *Theorizing masculinities*. Thousand Oaks, CA: Sage.

Chang, J. (2007). *Can't stop won't stop: A history of the hip-hop generation*. New York, NY: St. Martin's Press.

Cheema, J. R., & Galluzzo, G. (2013). Analyzing the gender gap in math achievement: Evidence from a large-scale US sample. *Research in Education, 90*(1), 98–112.

Cho, S., & Westley, R. (2002). Historicizing critical race theory's cutting edge: Key movements that performed the theory. In F. Valdes, M. J. Culp, & P. A. Harris (Eds.), *Crossroads directions, and a new critical race theory* (pp. 32–70). Philadelphia, PA: Temple University Press.

Clark, R., Harris, A., White-Smith, A. K., Allen, R. W., & Ray, B. A. (2010). The positive effects of after-school programs for African American Male Development and Educational Progress. In E. W. Johnson Jr. (Ed.), *Social work with African American males* (pp. 117–147). New York, NY: Oxford University Press.

Coates, T. (2013). How stand your ground relates to George Zimmerman. *The Atlantic*. Published July 16, 2013 and Retrieved November 20, 2017 from https://www.theatlantic.com/national/archive/2013/07/how-stand-your-ground-relates-to-george-zimmerman/277829/

Coates, T. (2015). *Between the world and me*. New York, NY: Spiegel and Grau.

Coates, T. (2017). *We Were Eight Years in Power: An American Tragedy*. New York, NY: One World/Ballantine.

Corbado, D. W. (2011). Critical what? *Connecticut Law Review, 34*(5), 1595–1643.

Crenshaw, W. K. (1995). Mapping the margins: Intersectionality, identity politics, and violence against women of color. In W. K. Crenshaw, N. Gotanda, G. Peller, & K. Thomas (Eds.), *Critical race theory: The key writings that formed the movement* (pp. 357–383). New York, NY: The New Press.

Crenshaw, W. K. (2011). Twenty years of critical race theory: Looking back to move forward. *Connecticut Law Review, 43*(5), 1255–1346.

Davis, J. E. (2006). Research at the margin: Mapping masculinity and mobility of African-American high school dropouts. *International Journal of Qualitative Studies in Education, 19*(3), 289–305.

Delgado, R. (2000). Storytelling for oppositionists and others: A plea for narrative. In R. Delgado & J. Stefancic (Eds.), *Critical race theory: The cutting edge*. Philadelphia, PA: Temple University Press.

Delgado, R., & Stefancic, J. (2001). *Critical race theory: An introduction*. New York, NY: New York University Press.

Dyson, M. E. (2005). *Is Bill Cosby Right?: Or Has the Black Middle Class Lost Its Mind?*. New York, NY: Civitas Books.

Eckholm, E., & Apuzzo, M. (2015). Darrien Wilson is cleared of rights violations in Fergusson Shooting. *The New York Times*. Published March 4, 2015 and Retrieved November 20, 2017 from https://www.nytimes.com/2015/03/05/us/darren-wilson-is-cleared-of-rights-violations-in-ferguson-shooting.html

Edwards, H. (2000). Crisis of black athletes on the eve of the 21st century. *Society, 37*(3), 9–13.

Eitle, T., & Eitle, D. (2002). Race, cultural capital, and the educational effects of participation in sports. *Sociology of Education, 75*, 123–146.

Ellis, E. M. (2001). The impact of race and gender on graduate school socialization, satisfaction with doctoral study, and commitment to degree completion. *Western Journal of Black Studies, 25*(1), 30.

Ferguson, A. A. (2000). *Bad boys: Public schools in the making of black masculinity*. Ann Arbor, MI: University of Michigan Press.

Fischer, R. (2004). Standardization to account for cross-cultural response bias: A classification of score adjustment procedures and review of research in JCCP. *Journal of Cross-Cultural Psychology, 35*(3), 263–282.

Foster, M. (1995). African American teachers and culturally relevant pedagogy. In J. A. Banks & C. A. M. Banks (Eds.), *Handbook of research on multicultural education* (pp. 570–581). New York, NY: Macmillan.

Fultz, M., & Brown, A. (2008). Historical perspectives on African American males as subjects of education policy. *American Behavioral Scientist, 51*(7), 854–871.

Garibaldi, M. A. (2007). The educational status of African American males in the 21st century. *Journal of Negro Education, 76*(3), 324–333.

Gibbs, J. T. (1988). *Young, black and male in America: An endangered species*. New York, NY: Auburn House.

Giroux, H. A. (2001). *Theory and resistance in education: Towards a pedagogy for the opposition* (Rev. ed.). Westport, CT: Bergin & Garvey.

Gotanda, N. (1991). A critique of "our constitution is color-blind." *Stanford Law Review, 44*, 1–69.

Hall, L., & Burns, L. (2009). Identity development and mentoring in doctoral education. *Harvard Educational Review, 79*(1), 49–70.

Haney Lopez, I. F. (1996). *White by law: The legal construction of race*. New York, NY: New York University Press.

Harper, S. R. (2012). *Black male student success in higher education: A report from the National Black Male College Achievement Study*. University of Pennsylvania, Graduate School of Education, Center for the Study of Race and Equity in Education.

Harper, S. R., & Davis III, C. H. (2012). They (don't) care about education: A counternarrative on Black male students' responses to inequitable schooling. *The Journal of Educational Foundations, 26*(1/2), 103–120.

Harris, A. P. (2001). Foreword. In R. Delgado & J. Stefancic, J. (Eds.), *Critical race theory: An introduction* (pp. xvii–xxi). New York, NY: New York University Press.

Harris, C. I. (1995). Whiteness as property. In K. Crenshaw, N. Gotanda, & K. Thomas (Eds.), *Critical race theory: The key writings that formed the movement* (pp. 276–291). New York, NY: New Press.

Harris, P. C. (2012). The sports participation effect on educational attainment of Black males. *Education and Urban Society, 46* (5), 507 – 521.

Helms, J. E. (1992). Why is there no study of cultural equivalence in standardized cognitive ability testing? *American Psychologist, 47*(9), 1083 - 1101.

Holzman, M. (2012). National Summary. In J. Jackson, A. Beaudry, E. Dexter, & T. K.Watson (Eds.), *The urgency of now: The Schott 50 state report on public education and Black males 2012* (pp. 1–56). Cambridge, MA: Schott Foundation of Public Education. Retrieved November 16, 2017 from http://blackboysreport.org/bbreport2012.pdf

Horsford, S. D., & Grosland, T. (2013). Badges of inferiority: The racialization of achievement in US education. In M. Lynn & A. D. Dixson (Eds.), *Handbook of critical race theory in education* (pp. 153–166). New York, NY: Routledge.

Howard, T. C. (2014). *Black male (D): Peril and promise in the education of African American males*. New York, NY: Teachers College Press.

Hutchinson, E. O. (2006). *The assassination of the black male image*. New York, NY: Touchstone.

Jeffries, D., & Jeffries, R. (2017). Marxist Materialism and Critical Race Theory: A Comparative Analysis of Media and Cultural Influence on the Formation of Stereotypes and Proliferation of Police Brutality against Black Men. *Spectrum: A Journal on Black Men, 5*(2), 1–22.

Kannapel, P. J., Clements, S. K., Taylor, D., & Hibpshman, T. (2005). Inside the black box of high-performing high-poverty schools. *Report, Prichard Committee for Academic Excellence*.

Kincheloe, J. (2005). *Critical pedagogy*. New York, NY: Peter Lang.

Kunjufu, J. (1990). *Countering the conspiracy to destroy Black boys* (Vol. 3). Chicago, IL: African American Images.

Kunjufu, J. (2005). *Countering the conspiracy to destroy Black boys*. Chicago, IL: African American Images.

Ladson-Billings, G., & Tate, W. F. I. (2006). Toward a critical race theory of education. In A. D. Dixson & C. K. Rousseau (Eds.), *Critical race theory in education: All God's children got a song* (pp. 11–30). New York, NY: Routledge Taylor & Francis Group.

Leavy, W. (1983, August). Is the Black male an endangered species? *Ebony*, pp. 41–46.

Lewis, T. (2003). The surveillance of post-columbine schools. *Review of Education, Pedagogy and Cultural Studies Taylor and Francis, 25*(4), 335–355.

Lindsay, V. (2015) "The class that race built: Putting race at the center of a higher education course to challenge post-racialism in the United States and Brazil." *Journal of Higher Education: Theory and Practice: 15,*(7), 11–24.

Lindsay, V. (2013). *"They Schools Ain't Teachin Us": Black males, resistance, and education at Uhuru High School* (Doctoral dissertation). Retrieved from Proquest database. University of Illinois at Chicago.

Lowery, W. (2016). *They can't kill us all: Ferguson, Baltimore, and a new era in America's racial justice movement*. New York, NY: Little, Brown, and Company.

Lynn, M. (1999). Toward a critical race pedagogy: A research note. *Urban Education, 33*(5), 606–626.

Madhubuti, H. R. (2006). *Yellow Black: The first twenty-one years of a poet's life*. Chicago, IL: Third World Press.

McAlpine, L., & Norton, J. (2006). Reframing our approach to doctoral programs: An integrative framework for action and research. *Higher Education Research & Development, 25*(1), 3–17.

McCallum, C. (2017). Giving back to the community: How African Americans envision utilizing their PhD. *The Journal of Negro Education, 86*(2), 138–153.

Noguera, P. (2001, December 1). Joaquin's dilemma: Understanding the link between racial identity and school-related behaviors. *Motion Magazine*. Retrieved March 12, 2013 from http://www.inmotionmagazine.com/er/pnjoaqref.html

Noguera, P. A. (2003). The trouble with Black boys: The role and influence of environmental and cultural factors on the academic performance of African American males. *Urban education, 38*(4), 431–459.

Omi, M., & Winant, H. (1994). *Racial formation in the United States: From the 1960s to the 1990s*. New York, NY: Routledge.

Parham, T., & McDavis, R. (1987). Black men, an endangered species: Who's really pulling the trigger? *Journal of Counseling and Development, 66*, 24–27.

Parker, L., & Lynn, M. (2002). What's race got to do with it? Critical race theory's conflicts with and connections to qualitative research methodology and epistemology. *Qualitative Inquiry, 8*(1), 7–22.

Porter, M. (1997). *Kill them before they grow: Misdiagnosis of African American boys in American classrooms*. Chicago, IL: African American Images.

Roberts, D. (2011). *Fatal invention: How science, politics, and big business re-create race in the twenty-first century*. New York, NY: The New Press.

Scafidi, T., & Bui, K. (2010). Gender similarities in math performance from middle school through high school. *Journal of Instructional Psychology, 37*(3), 252–256.

Scott, S. V. (2017). *The struggle is real: Black Doctoral Students' perceptions aspiring to the professoriate* (Doctoral dissertation). Philadelphia, PA: Temple University.

Smith, D. M. (2016). *Invisible man got the whole world watching: A young Black man's education*. New York, NY: Nation Books.

Solórzano, D. G., & Yosso, T. J. (2002). Critical race methodology: Counter-storytelling as an analytical framework for education research. *Qualitative Inquiry*, 8(1), 23–44.

Solórzano, D. G., & Yosso, J. T. (2016). Critical race methodology: Counter-storytelling as an analytical framework for educational research. In E. Taylor, D. Gillborn, & G. Ladson-Billings (Eds.), *Foundations of critical race theory in education* (pp. 127–153). New York, NY: Routledge.

Stovall, D. (2013). "Fightin' the Devil 24/7": Context, community and critical race praxis in education. In M. Lynn & A. D. Dixson (Eds.), *Handbook of critical race theory in education* (pp. 289–301). New York, NY: Routledge.

Strickland, W. (1989, November). Our men in crisis: Together we must meet the enormous challenge facing Black men. *Essence*, pp. 49–52.

Swaine, J., Laughland, O., Lartey, J., & McCarthy, C. (2015). *Young Black men killed by US police at highest rate in year of 1,134 deaths.* Retrieved November 16, 2017 from https://www.theguardian.com/us-news/2015/dec/31/the-counted-police-killings-2015-young-black-men

Travis, R. (2013). Rap music and the empowerment of today's youth: Evidence in everyday music listening, music therapy, and commercial rap music. *Child and Adolescent Social Work Journal*, 30(2), 139–167.

Tuchman, G. (1999). *Drills, new security measures mark return to schools.* CNN Retrieved on December 11, 2017 from http://edition.cnn.com/US/9908/16/school.safety/

Vaught, E. S. (2011). *Racism, public schooling and the entrenchment of white supremacy: A critical race ethnography.* Albany, NY: State University of New York Press.

Winant, H. (2001). *The world is a ghetto: Race and democracy since World War II.* New York, NY: Basic Books.

Yosso, J. T. (2006). *Critical race counterstories along the Chicano/Chicano educational pipeline.* New York, NY: Routledge Taylor and Francis Group.

Young, A. A. (2004). *The minds of marginalized Black men: Making sense of mobility, opportunity and future life chances.* Princeton, NJ: Princeton University Press.

Zimmerman, M. A., Eisman, A. B., Reischl, T. M., Morrel-Samuels, S., Stoddard, S., Miller, A. L., Hutchnison, P., Franzen, S., & Rupp, L. (2017). Youth Empowerment Solutions: Evaluation of an after-school program to engage middle school students in community change. *Health Education & Behavior*, 45 (1), 20–31.

INDEX